FRASER:
Not a Private Matter

'The grace of God, though given in a
way which is intimately personal,
is not a private matter.'

JOHN TALLACH

catherine gyrart.

FRASER:
Not a Private Matter

Fraser Tallach

with

John Tallach and
David Tallach

THE BANNER OF TRUTH TRUST

THE BANNER OF TRUTH TRUST
3 Murrayfield Road, Edinburgh EH12 6EL, UK
P.O. Box 621, Carlisle, PA 17013, USA

*

© John and David Tallach 2003

ISBN 0 85151 847 8

*

Typeset in 12 /15 pt Goudy Old Style by
Initial Typesetting Services, Dalkeith
Printed and bound in Great Britain
by the Cromwell Press Ltd.,
Trowbridge, Wilts.

Contents

Illustrations

Frontispiece: Fraser, graduation in Arts, University of Edinburgh.

Between pages 54 and 55:
    Family group, Tighnabruaich, 1951:
        Back row – Fraser, Rev. James Tallach, Elizabeth Tallach, Andrew;
        Front row – John, James, Cameron.
    Fraser in Canada, 1965.
    Fraser and Mother.
    Fraser, John and James.

Dedication

This book is dedicated to Cameron, whose gift of a kidney to his brother Fraser was the means of adding nearly thirty years to his life.

Also to Fraser's Aunt Helen, who looked after him as a boy (1951–3), and kept house for him from time to time during his ministry. This became particulary meaningful during the latter years of Fraser's life. Her unselfish commitment to her nephew has left the whole family in her debt.

We also wish to mention the Highland Hospice, Inverness, where Fraser died, 3 November 1998. One third of any royalties from the sale of this book will be used to support the ongoing work of the Hospice.

JOHN AND DAVID TALLACH

A Word of Explanation

Fraser was the second of five sons, of whom I am the youngest.

After Fraser died in 1998, a substantial piece of writing was found among his papers. Written in 1992, this manuscript was based on a diary he had kept when passing through a life-threatening illness in the 1960s.

Fraser's executor (our brother James) asked me to look at this manuscript. Typical of Fraser, it revealed his unique personality, but was in need of editing. It needed more structure and less detail. The privilege of editing Fraser's manuscript has been shared between me and my son David, who had a deep appreciation of his uncle.

David also wrote some poems about Fraser, and I provided background material. When the publishers saw this background material, they suggested that it be developed, believing that this would help readers to set Fraser's own story in context.

The book, as now presented, follows the pattern suggested by the publishers. Part One gives some family background and brings events up to the point at which Fraser's story begins. Fraser's own story appears in Part Two. Part Three provides a brief conclusion, in relation both to Fraser and to our mother, whose life was so entwined with Fraser's that the story of his life was to an extent the story of hers. This section also includes the poems which David wrote about his uncle.

As I thought about God's care over those whose experiences are told in this book it occurred to me that the grace of God, though given in a way which is intimately personal, is not a private matter. Rather it is a public statement about himself which God makes to the world, through the lives of those to whom this grace is given. That is why we have called this book *Fraser: Not a Private Matter*.

JOHN TALLACH
The Manse
Cromarty
Scotland
October 2003

Part One

FAMILY BACKGROUND

1

Forebears

Our family roots lie deep in the history of the Scottish Highlands.

On our mother's side, at least one forebear experienced the horrors of the Clearances at first hand. Our great-, great-, great-, great- grandfather was moved off his land to make room for sheep. Along with other destitute folk, he settled on a rough piece of ground at Tore in Easter Ross. There were no crops to harvest that year and the spot became known in Gaelic, for years after that first hard winter, as 'the hill of hunger'.

On our father's side, our grandfather was born in Easter Ross in 1858. When he was thirty years old, he and his wife moved to Dornoch, Sutherland, where he took over a small business. Our father, one of eight children, was born in 1896 and was called James. The whole family lived in rooms above the shop. As he grew up, Father and his older brother John would sometimes stand at an open upstairs window and try to knock off the hats of whoever passed along the pavement below. On one occasion, Father managed to dislodge the hat of the local policeman, who then chased him without success for two miles across the Dornoch Links. The Links was also a source of income. Father could earn up to sixpence a time there in the summer, acting as caddy for the wealthy visiting golfers.

Grandfather had been brought up in the Free Church. In 1893, when some left the Free Church to form the Free Presbyterian Church, Grandfather was at first unsure what to do. After a pause, he joined the F. P. Church. It was a church which took a firm, conservative stance in matters of doctrine and practice, tending to point out the failings of other denominations which did not share its outlook in every respect. Personally, Andrew Tallach had a reputation as a man of prayer and a man of peace.

On Sundays he took the English services at the F. P. Church in Dornoch, but during the week he nursed along his small business. Perhaps he was too soft-hearted to be a businessman. He found it difficult to pursue those customers for payment who were evidently struggling to make ends meet. Also, he had a partner in the business whose duties included taking money to the bank. One day this partner disappeared. Grandfather went to the bank and discovered that the takings, which he had believed were being deposited in the bank, had in fact been going into his partner's pocket. Grandfather's main concern was, to pay off any debts which the business owed. His wife had a small amount of savings, and they agreed that these should be cashed so that all the creditors would be paid. This left them penniless, but free from debt.

In 1906 Grandfather applied to the F. P. Church to be employed as a lay preacher. The church told him to take responsibility for the services in Lochinver, a village of out-standing beauty on the west coast of Sutherland.

This presented a difficulty. Grandfather had no money to pay the fare for the public transport from Lairg to Lochinver.

However, he had to travel if he was to take up his new appointment. He got on the horse drawn transport, complete with his wife, his family and his possessions. In the course of that journey, one wheel went into a hole in the road, something gave way and the vehicle went on its side. As a gesture of good will to the passengers who had suffered this trauma, the company running the transport allowed them all to travel free that day.

After serving the church for four years in Lochinver, Grandfather was told to move south. This time he was to look after the F. P. congregation on the island of Raasay, between the west coast of the Scottish mainland and the island of Skye.

Raasay was to become Grandfather's home until he died there in 1923. His stay on this island, with its wonderful views of the Cuillins of Skye, thus included the years of the First World War. Throughout that time, our father and two of our uncles were away from home on active service, two in the army and one in the navy. There was one day in each week when Grandfather walked through the woods above his home, looking for firewood. In the evening, he would come down from the woods with a few branches. Actually, his main occupation on these days was, to pray for his three sons who were away at the war. One day he came home with a light step and his wife asked him why. He replied:

> I was thinking of the three men in the book of Daniel who came through the fiery furnace. They came through that trial without even the smell of the fire on their clothes. I believe that God gave me that verse when I was up in the woods, praying for John and James and Anderson. And I believe that all three of them will come through the war unscathed.

His faith was completely vindicated. Uncle John, who after the war went as a missionary to Africa, once cut his finger when opening a tin. This prompted the comment:

> I got a worse injury from opening that tin than I ever got from all that I came through in the trenches in France.

Returning to the forebears on our mother's side, Mother's father, Samuel Fraser, was brought up on a small farm at Tore. His mother seems to have been a very committed Christian. She valued the preaching of Dr Kennedy of Dingwall so much that she used to walk each Sunday from Tore to Alcaig, from where she got a ferry over to a point below Dingwall (a round walk of about fifteen miles). On more than one occasion she walked to attend the 'communion season' at Creich, above Bonar Bridge. (Traditional communion seasons in the Highlands were times when many gathered for services, from a Thursday to a Monday, arranged around the communion itself held on a Sunday morning.) The walk to Creich would have involved a distance of about forty miles each way. Of one such weekend she said that she and others had experienced the presence of God to such a degree that they had not slept a wink over the whole weekend. Her father spoke to her about leaving Donald, Samuel and all the other children for such a prolonged period. She replied that such times helped to satisfy her thirst for the gospel and for fellowship with other believers; and that, when she was away, the older children helped to look after the younger ones.

Her father was not a man to be trifled with. Donald Duff had first been awakened to a sense of his spiritual need through the preaching of Dr Macdonald of Ferintosh, 'The

Apostle of the North'. He remained a layman, but as Archibald Auld wrote:

> Possessing a mind exceptionally able and acute, his expositions of Scripture were quite remarkable for their insight and spirituality . . . This power, in addition to his solid and judicious character, made him helpful to many, and gave him a distinct position in the church.[1]

There were twelve brothers and sisters in our grandfather Samuel's family. As the children grew up, they left home one by one, most of them for Glasgow, about two hundred miles away. Donald, Samuel's older brother, was one of the first to leave. On the day chosen for his departure he ate a large lunch, mounted his penny-farthing, and set off for the big city. Unfortunately there was a bend at the bottom of the road which sloped down from the farm. Donald failed to negotiate the bend, landed face down in a field, and was sustained by his large lunch in a way different from what he had planned. In fairness to Donald, penny-farthings were notoriously difficult to ride. They had a huge wheel at the front, and a tiny wheel at the rear. The seat was placed above the big wheel. You could build up a good speed on these primitive machines, but they were very unstable and if you hit a pot-hole it was a long way to the ground.

When the time came for Samuel (Grandfather) to leave home, he also got on his bike and made his way to Glasgow to train as a draper.

---

[1] Archibald Auld, *Memorials of Caithness Ministers* (Edinburgh: Henderson, 1911), p. 291. *Gleanings of Highland Harvest*, by Murdoch Campbell, (Dingwall: Religious Bookroom, 1969), also contains a chapter on Donald Duff.

On his first holiday, he cycled back north to the Black Isle. It was during this visit that he met the daughter of a gamekeeper who lived above Munlochy called Elizabeth Cameron. Samuel continued with his plan for a cycling holiday on the west coast, and visited Skye. However, once there, he found that he had left his heart back in the Black Isle. He cut short his trip to Skye, pedalled furiously back east, and spent the rest of his holiday seeing as much as he could of the gamekeeper's daughter. They were married in 1910. The photo of their wedding is stunning, with large expensive hats signalling a last flamboyant flowering of a dying age.

Our mother was born in Glasgow in 1911, and named Elizabeth Duff Fraser, the middle name being in honour of her great-grandfather. The following year the family moved back north to Ross-shire, settling in Strathpeffer (five miles west of Dingwall) where her father had bought a draper's business.

2

Mother's Conversion

In the early days in Strathpeffer, Samuel Fraser used to cycle on Sundays to attend the F. P. services in Dingwall. As there was no transport for the rest of the family, they normally attended the services in the Free Church in Strathpeffer. It was on one of these occasions that Mother heard the Rev. Kenneth MacRae[2] preach on John 3:36, 'He who believes on the Son has everlasting life: and he who does not believe the Son shall not see life; but the wrath of God abides on him.' Mother was only twelve years old when she heard that sermon in 1923, but she could remember the details clearly when she recounted that experience as long afterwards as January 2001:

> He pressed on us so powerfully the duty of believing in Christ. 'Are you willing to have Jesus?' he asked. 'He is willing to have you.' I cried when I got home from that service.
>
> *What was upsetting me?* I think it was my longing to have Christ. Probably I was converted then, but I went through a long period of questioning, and did

[2] See *Diary of Kenneth MacRae* (Edinburgh: Banner of Truth, 1980).

not find peace until years later. My question was, 'What does it mean to believe?' One day, as I was washing dishes, I got help from the words of Acts 16:31: 'Believe on the Lord Jesus Christ, and you will be saved.' Light shone into my heart and I realized the simplicity of the gospel.

I got help from Mr Macfarlane right from when he came to Dingwall.[3] I would be moved to tears at times. I was always looking for something. But things did not become completely clear to me until after that, when I read a chapter in a book written by Spurgeon on *Faith – What Is It?*

There is a tie-up here between Mother and her great-grandfather Donald Duff, after whom she was called. In 1870 Donald Duff met C. H. Spurgeon, when that outstanding minister came north from London to preach at the opening of the new Free Church in Dingwall. Donald Duff had a critical streak in him but he was profoundly impressed, both by Spurgeon's company and by his preaching. He had been reading his printed sermons for years; now he was thrilled to feel for himself the full impact of Spurgeon's simple, deep, passionate preaching. It is interesting that, sixty years later, the writings of the same minister were to be crucial in Mother's experience, helping her to find peace through personal faith in Christ.

[3] The Rev. D. A. Macfarlane came to Dingwall as minister of the Free Presbyterian Church in 1930 and continued there until he retired in 1973.

3

Courtship –
Elizabeth Fraser and
James Tallach

DEAR MISS FRASER,

I am writing to you to make confession of theft . . .

So begins one of the earliest letters between our parents.
Father had been visiting the Fraser home in Strathpeffer,
had pocketed a photo of his future wife during that visit, and
was now writing to confess his misdeed. However, instead of
expressing regret, he wrote, 'The oftener I look at it the more
inclined I am to rejoice that I have it.'

On another early visit to Strathpeffer, looking at his
intended one night from the other side of the fire, our future
father suggested that it would be nice to see the beauties of the
village in the light of the moon. Mother hung her head
modestly, saying nothing. Her Uncle Donald (the one who
came off the penny-farthing at Tore) was in the room at the
time and, glaring at the visitor, got up and went to the kitchen
in search of his boots. As he pulled them on he complained to

his sister in law, 'That fellow is wanting to go out for a walk. I suppose I'd better take him.' It was a cold, frosty night; but that is not the only reason why that walk was cut short.

In May 1931, Father was inducted as minister of the F. P. congregation in Kames, Kyles of Bute. Afterwards, he wrote off to Strathpeffer with a report on how things had gone.

He also sent a couple of post cards, 'so that you will see what kind of place I have landed in. It is beautiful – that is, as beautiful as it can be to me, without you. I would think the Bass Rock beautiful if you were there.'

James Tallach was fifteen years older than Betty Fraser. By August 1931, he felt that they had discussed their future long enough and he wrote to say, 'I want to know if you will marry me or not.'

Soon after that, Mother was cycling along a country road near Strathpeffer with this letter in her pocket. Turning everything over in her mind as she pedalled along, she felt a desire to commit all the huge issues involved to God in prayer. The road was deserted, so she got off her bike and went into the woods to pray. While she was praying she realized something which became a significant factor in her future decision. One of the reasons why she felt drawn towards this offer of marriage was that, as a minister's wife, she would have an opportunity to serve God as she shared in her husband's work.

Mother did not actually agree to Father's proposal for some time after that, but her reply to his letter must have indicated some movement in that direction. When Father had read her response he wrote back,

> Well, that's quite a refreshing drink. It reminds me of
> the rum we used to get in the trenches just at dawn,

after a long dreary night on the look out. Half frozen in body, and wholly frozen in spirit – then the rum acted just like magic, going straight to the centre of the heart and thawing and warming up things beautifully.

As well as writing about the place, Father also referred in his letters to the people: the forty people who attended the midweek service, even on a wet Wednesday evening: his housekeeper Amy, and the members of his family who came to stay with him from time to time.

His brother Anderson came, and they stayed up half the night talking about scenes and events from their childhood in Dornoch, Lochinver and Raasay. In July 1932 his brother John came, with his wife Ann and young children. (John had gone to the F. P. Church Mission in Zimbabwe in 1924, and was now in Scotland for his first furlough.) In his letters around this time Father reports that he has been out in the evening shooting rabbits. 'I managed to get three, which is quite a consideration, with so many mouths to feed.' Father had completed an artificer's course at the Ordnance College, Woolwich. More significantly he had had experience of actual warfare, having enlisted with the 9th Highland Light Infantry on 12 May 1913, and having been on active service throughout the whole of the First War, not discharged until 25 April 1919. No doubt this was of merely academic interest to the Kames rabbits who ended their days in a pot in the manse, eaten by missionaries home from Africa.

During that summer of 1932, Father and his housekeeper Amy were once looking out over the manse garden and Amy commented:

'That hedge is growing very fast.'

Father replied,

'Not nearly fast enough!'

He was thinking of how slowly time seemed to pass, when the lady he loved was not yet there.

It was in August of that year that Mother finally made public profession of her faith in Christ. Father was so delighted. They were engaged a week later.

They were to be married on 3 January 1933, which happened to be Father's birthday. Looking forward to this most special of birthdays he wrote, 'I got a few good birthday presents when I was younger, but never anything so precious as this.' In another letter around this time he wrote, 'I love you . . . I can only thank you from the bottom of my heart, a heart that has somehow got considerably deeper since it knew you.'

4

Marriage

(This is told as Mother recounted it.)

Your father wrote me a letter when a communion passed and I did not become a member. I said to him, 'If only the Spirit would come.' But he said, 'The Spirit is already here.' I was 21 years old when I became a member. The Rev. M. Gillies preached that communion Sunday morning. It spoke to my heart. I felt my unworthiness, but then I thought of the words, 'Worthy is the Lamb that was slain.' It was a precious day. Your father and I became engaged a week after that.

We were to be married in the Columba Hotel, Inverness, on the third of January, 1933, by the Rev. Ewen MacQueen. It was a custom that you spent the last weekend before being married with your parents, so your father spent that week end in Raasay. He did not arrive on the Monday as we had expected. We did not know what was happening. Then a telegram arrived which said, *Delayed with storm.* The normal steamer had been unable to call at Raasay pier. My father said, 'If only I had an aeroplane, I would go and get them.' He went back and forth from Strathpeffer to the station at Achterneed to meet every train, but there was no news. (The phone lines on Raasay were down because of the storm.)

On Monday evening a cargo steamer managed to call at Raasay pier and your father and his brother Murdo got on it. It could not dock at Portree pier that night, but it was able to dock the next morning. They got a taxi to Kyleakin, and all the way to Inverness. Murdo's socks were soaking wet, and he hung them out of the window to dry, but they blew away. At one point the taxi went over a bump and Murdo's head hit the roof.

We did not know anything about what was happening. It was the morning of the wedding, but we did not know if there was to be a wedding or not. I was sorry for my mother, but I felt a peace. I asked my father to sing Psalm 121, and we set off from Strathpeffer for Inverness. When we arrived at the hotel there was a telegram saying, *Arriving two hours late*. I was put up to a bedroom. My Auntie Maggie had a lodger in Glasgow, and she said to me that this was a good chance to marry her lodger! Then I caught sight of your father getting out of the taxi. It was hardly a dignified arrival. Your uncle Murdo had a gash on his head, and your father's white scarf was flying in the breeze. But it was such a relief, and such a thrill.

5

Kames

So, in January 1933, Betty Fraser became the wife of the F. P. minister in the congregation of Kames. The Kames manse was to be her home for the next nineteen years. Here she was to share in caring for the congregation and the community. Here she was to bring her five boys into the world – Andrew, Fraser (born on 13 May 1938, James, Cameron and me. (I think our parents had hoped that I would be a girl!)

Fraser commented once that one of the early memories of his childhood was the sound of Mother's footsteps as she sped round (while the rest of the family were still in bed) doing the household chores. She was tall, was built as she used to say with big bones, and was very strong. (Once, when Andrew was on the verge of contesting her authority, he took the precaution first of feeling Mother's biceps and backed off with the comment, 'A woman should never have muscles like that!')

One memory of his childhood in the Kames manse which is retained by our brother Cameron is connected with prayer. He had come across a bird's nest, and had inadvertently disturbed it. A passing adult said that, because of this, the mother bird would not come back to that nest. Cameron remembers Mother praying about that, asking God to keep the mother bird from abandoning her chicks. It helped to bring home to him at an early age the fact that prayer is relevant to every aspect of our daily lives.

As a minister's wife, Mother demonstrated her commitment to the gospel of Christ and to the coming of God's kingdom by prayer, by supporting the preaching of the gospel, by promoting fellowship among Christians, by identifying with those who were passing through trouble, and by encouraging those who were not yet Christians to 'taste and see that God is good'.

Her greatest desire was, to see her own children come to personal faith in Christ. In Fraser's case this happened in 1950, when he was eleven years old. Mother was reading to us from a book for children called, *Peep of Day.* The author was explaining the significance of the death of Christ. Fraser said, years later:

> I was so deeply moved that I went next door into the kitchen. I still remember the exact spot where I was standing when the meaning of the death of Christ flashed on my mind. What I had been trying to do for myself, Christ had already done. I cried that night, not from sorrow but from relief.

School was a mile and a half away from Kames, in Tighnabruaich. This involved daily walks which could seem very long to a small child. In the autumn, we trailed our feet through the piles of leaves which lay beside the road. In the winter, we could slide on the pools where the water had frozen solid.

There was no secondary school in Tighnabruaich. When our oldest brother Andrew had finished Primary School, he went (with the help of a bursary) to Keil Boarding School in Dumbarton. In 1951, when it came to Fraser's turn to move on to Secondary School, he went to Dingwall. (Mother's parents, and her younger sister, Helen, had moved from Strathpeffer to Dingwall in 1946. Her father had died there in 1949.) In Dingwall, looked after by his grandmother and his Aunt Helen, Fraser attended Dingwall Academy.

6

Stornoway

In the autumn of 1952, Father accepted a call to become minister of the F. P. congregation in Stornoway, Lewis, in the Outer Hebrides. This did not immediately affect Fraser, who stayed on in Dingwall to complete that school year. But in the summer of 1953 he left Dingwall to join the rest of the family in 24 James Street, Stornoway.

Father's ministry in Stornoway, though it would last about a third as long as his ministry in Kames, was to prove meaningful to many people. He had three services every Sunday. His own congregation appreciated his ministry, some of them coming to faith in Christ for the first time through his preaching. Members of other churches also came on occasion to hear him preach on the Sunday afternoon, when there was no service in their own church.

I particularly remember the services on Sunday evening. There was a simplicity and a directness about the preaching. There was a compassion and an earnestness which, on occasion, meant that the whole service was very moving. Mother would always look back on this as a special period in her life. The blessing which accompanied Father's preaching, folk being brought into the church, the warmth of fellowship among Christians; to Mother, these things were bread from heaven.

Fraser was a very competent athlete and excelled on the sports field. However he also worked hard at his studies, and in 1956 he was accepted as a medical student by Edinburgh University. Scientific detail fascinated him, and he would always retain an interest in the study of medicine. However, as he got into the second year of his medical studies, a problem arose. Fraser began to feel that he was being called to the ministry. He fought against this, refusing to believe that he had the requisite gifts, and for some months the conflict in his mind became so severe that he could not concentrate on his work. In the end he had to give in to the rising conviction that God had called him, not to be a doctor but to be a minister of the gospel. Accordingly, he changed from the Faculty of Medicine to the Faculty of Arts and studied towards a Master of Arts degree.

One Wednesday evening, in the summer of 1959, Mother and Father were coming back from a service in Swordale, some miles out of Stornoway. The road home passed beside a beach in an area called The Braigh. Father pulled the black Ford Popular over and switched off the engine. Nothing could be heard but the sound of the waves. Father put his hand on hers and quoted the words of a poem:

> *Break, break, break,*
> *On thy cold grey stones, O sea!*
> *And I would that my tongue could utter*
> *The thoughts that arise in me.*
>
> *And the stately ships go on*
> *To their haven under the hill;*
> *But O for the touch of a vanish'd hand,*
> *And the sound of a voice that is still!*

Break, break, break
At the foot of thy crags, O sea!
But the tender grace of a day that is dead
Will never come back to me.[1]

Mother said, 'Come on, James. We can't wait here. There are people coming to the house and I need to be back to get tea ready.' However he refused to be hurried. He went on to say, in a way which she would always treasure, how much she meant to him. Then he switched on the ignition, pulled the starter, and BJS 662 was on her way again.

Later that same year, Mother was dusting a door in the manse when a thought came into her mind, *What would you do if James was taken away? You would be helpless and useless.* There was no apparent reason for this negative thought, but she felt the force of it deeply. Then the words from the end of Psalm 23 came to her:

Goodness and mercy all my life
Shall surely follow me.
And in God's house for evermore
My dwelling place shall be.

She took comfort from these words in two ways. She felt sure that the goodness and mercy of God would come behind her to support her, and she felt that God would also go before her to provide for her in a way which could never be taken away.

Towards the end of that year my brother Andrew, who had gone in 1956 to work in agriculture in Malawi, came home with his wife Beth for their first furlough. He told me stories

[1] Alfred Lord Tennyson, *Selected Poems*, Penguin Classics, 1991, p. 119.

about life in Africa, which helped to pass the time as I recovered from measles. Then, suddenly, illness of a more serious nature visited our home. Father felt unwell one day and stayed in bed for a few hours but I remember him getting up in the afternoon and shaving in front of the mirror in the living room. Mother came through from the kitchen and tried to persuade him not to take a service which he was due to take that evening in Sandwick, outside Stornoway. Father's reply was, 'Who knows? It may be the last chance I'll get to preach the gospel.'

He spoke with feeling that night from the words at the beginning of Hosea chapter 6: 'Come, and let us return to the LORD.'

But, by three the next morning, the pain in Father's chest had become severe and Mother had to send for the doctor. I slept through all that, but in the morning I was wakened by Andrew.

'Father has been unwell during the night,' he said, 'and he wants to see each of us. He has spoken to Cameron, and now he wants to see you.'

Father was lying flat in bed, his face was white and his hand was cold. But there was a peace and joy in that room which one could almost reach out and touch. Father spoke to me about Jesus, and asked if I wanted to have him for my own Saviour. I believed that I could say, 'Yes', but I did not have the strength to say anything. I felt the pain of an impending parting. But there was something else in that room, something which was stronger than death, which took the bitterness of death away. Looking back, the best way to describe it is in the words of Scripture: 'Then the saying that is written will come true: *Death has been swallowed up in victory.*'

Believing that he was dying, Father was sorry not to be able to speak with Fraser or James, who were both in Edinburgh. But, speaking privately to Mother, he said:

> It means a lot to me that Fraser has professed his faith in Christ. That has been a great comfort to me.

Father actually survived that first attack, so both Fraser and James did see him again as he lay in a side ward of the Lewis Hospital. On 12 January 1960, however, he had a second attack from which he did not recover.

Had Fraser been at home at the beginning of December, and again in the middle of January, he would have heard nothing from Father, looking back from his deathbed over his ministry, to discourage him from the vocation to which he too now felt himself to be called.

'My happiest times have been in preaching the gospel,' Father said. 'Every remembrance of Jesus makes me smile.'

When the time for parting came, Mother was given grace to a degree which left her astonished. Looking back years later, she wrote:

> I was privileged to share him his triumphant entrance into glory. I say 'share' for it was fellowship in the gospel of a very deep and real kind, the Lord filling our hearts with his presence which gave joy even though about to part. I remember a distinct longing to go with him – not at all that I wanted to leave my dear family – but to continue this wonderful close - ness of spirit to each other through the Saviour.

Women attended only the first part of funerals in those days. Mother was in a car parked beside the road out of Stornoway, as the cortège passed on its way from the church where Father had preached for over seven years to Sandwick Cemetery. A light drizzle began to fall as we walked slowly along, the family immediately behind the coffin. As an unreasonable fourteen year old, I grudged to see the drops of rain spoil the bright polish on the coffin lid.

Mother had given us a verse to think of that day, to help us cope when we turned to leave our father in that spot overlooking the entrance to Stornoway harbour. The words were from Micah 2:10, 'Arise and depart, for this is not your rest.'

7

An Uncertain Future – and a Call to Canada

So, at 49 years of age, Mother suddenly had to face the future as a widow without a salary and without a home. The bank manager in Stornoway, discussing with her the fact that her late husband's assets at his death amounted to fifty pounds, looked across his large desk and asked,

'And was there *no insurance?*'

'No,' she replied, 'but "the Lord will provide".'

The bank manager lowered his gaze and said without conviction,

'Well, I hope he will.'

At that time Mother's mother and sister Helen were still living in Dingwall. So it was to Dingwall that we moved in the summer of 1960.

Mother tried to find work of one kind or another. For a time she took part-time work as a cleaner, which involved her travelling out by bus to Conon Bridge. After a few years she had the idea of starting to sell Christian books. In these days this was a somewhat novel idea. The assumption was that lack of demand would make it impossible to succeed in such a venture. But she found this work incomparably more to her taste. The contacts she made helped to satisfy the strong appetite for Christian fellowship which characterised her as it had done her grandmother (who had walked to attend communion seasons at Creich). Meeting Christians from other churches also helped to broaden her outlook. She herself was ready to admit that, given her church background, she *needed* these contacts to learn this increased openness.

During this period, Fraser finished his Arts degree and spent one year each with the three ministers who, in the F. P. Church, were appointed to give training to divinity students.

He finished this training in 1964, and came home to Dingwall in the early summer. By then in my last year in Dingwall Academy, I went over one evening to the sports field below the Academy to practise running a half mile. Fraser came with me for moral support, but he soon got tired of standing on the sidelines. He had not been on a running track for about ten years, but he asked me to time him as he ran a quarter mile. He did it in 61 seconds. I was very impressed.

In the course of that summer he was approached by the committee of the F. P. Church which had responsibility for the congregations connected with the church which lay overseas. This committee asked Fraser to consider going as a deputy of the church to Winnipeg, Canada. There was a small congregation of the F. P. Church there. This congregation had been bigger in the earlier days of the church, supported by folk who had emigrated from Scotland in search of work. (In fact, Father had served as a deputy in Winnipeg from 1926 to 1928.) By the 1960s the numbers had declined. Acting as pastor to this group would not be an easy task, but Fraser decided to take it on.

With this in view he was ordained in November 1964, in Inverness. The Rev. R. R. Sinclair of Wick preached on that occasion from Mark 16:20: 'Then the disciples went out and preached everywhere, and the Lord worked with them and confirmed his word by the signs that accompanied it.' There was real power with Mr Sinclair's preaching that evening. We were encouraged to believe that, when Fraser went to plough a lonely furrow in Winnipeg, he would not be alone.

Part Two

FRASER

Foreword

I have felt a reluctance to tell this story. It is like the hesitation one feels on entering a grotto. The sunlight outside is warm and pleasant, but as one advances there is only the gloom. In the same way, a person becoming ill is hemmed in to himself and his thoughts. Why burden the reader with these feelings? I have come out from the dark grotto into the light of day. Why should I wish to return?

My mother followed me through it all. Her interest was as unabated at the end as at the beginning; but then she cared for me because I was her son. I could not demand the same interest of a stranger. Now that I have emerged, is it not better to forget what is behind and to look forward?

The mention of 'forgetting' brings me back to the first time I attended church in Edinburgh after my kidney transplant. I should not think that Mr Campbell (the minister in the Free Presbyterian Church in Edinburgh at the time) had any idea that I would be back in church that particular day. He preached a sermon on the healing of the ten lepers. Christ had told them to go to the priest, and on the way there they felt life return to their dead limbs. Nine continued on. Perhaps ten did at first, wondering at the transformation and congratulating each other. But one stopped and retraced his steps. He did not rest until he had presented himself before his liberator and 'with a loud voice' given glory to God.

This is the only reason why I should retrace the different stages of my illness and recovery. I do it to discharge a debt of gratitude to those who brought me through it; and, above all, to God.

S. FRASER TALLACH

8

The Discovery

The bus thrummed onward through the night. On the skyline, one could see the jagged teeth of innumerable pine-tree tops etched against the pale blue sky. It was 1966, and I was travelling from Winnipeg in Canada, across the border to Chicago on a 24-hour journey. I could have gone by plane or train, but I preferred the bus because I could see the countryside more easily and meet a greater number of people. As a 28-year-old, I felt well able to cope with the rigours of the journey.

Suddenly, the uniform velvet-black of the forest was dotted with an array of lights. We were approaching a transport café and the bus slowed down and drew into the forecourt. Rather sleepily we stretched ourselves and tumbled out. I ordered a malt drink, not because I favoured the look of the thick sticky liquid but simply because I thought it would be less likely to keep me awake for the rest of the journey than either tea or coffee. We returned to our seats and the gentle roll of the bus as it pressed relentlessly on through the night soon lulled the passengers back to sleep. As we awoke, in the grey light of dawn, we were weaving among loops and coils of motorway, approaching the great city. The muted tones of the early morning light were replaced by the harsh glare of sun on concrete and steel; and the soporific drone of the bus was drowned in the clamour of a city which was awakening to a new day.

When the bus finally pulled into the terminus, I still had a few hours free before I caught my onward connection to Grand Rapids that afternoon. I decided to visit the city's Museum of Science and Industry, which turned out to be a gigantic, fascinating palace of wonders. There were demonstrations of satellites, of the weird properties of liquid nitrogen, and even a combined telephone and television. The museum testified to mankind's ingenuity and restless search for progress, to tremendous knowledge, magnificent skills and even greater ambition. However, all these things are subject to providence, and in the months and years ahead I was to become profoundly grateful for God-given new technology. But with only a quarter of the museum touched it was time to return to the centre of Chicago again.

On the way back to the bus, I began to feel dizzy. 'It's that malt drink', I thought, as I straightened my shoulders, determined not to give in to a passing squeamishness. But the dizziness got worse and by the time I reached the station I could hardly see. Wave after wave of nausea seemed to crash down upon me. I staggered along the platform to a waste-bin and vomited. As I lay bent over, I suddenly realized how awkward my situation was. Travelling any further was out of the question, and I was a sick man in a large, strange, foreign city.

A constant steam of people passed me, but not one face was known to me. I approached a street cleaner.

'Do you know where I could find a doctor?'

'No.' From the way he looked at me, he probably thought I was drunk.

[34]

'Is there a clinic, then?'

'Yes. If you go round the corner at the bottom of the street and wait at the bus stop, a bus will come that will take you there.' I followed his directions and waited for nearly an hour, only to discover that the bus did not run at that time of day. Seeing a hotel just across the road, I decided to book in for the night. The hotel porter was very kind.

'There is a doctor on the premises,' he said, 'I will get him to see you when he's free.' Armed with the doctor's prescription, I got some pills from a chemist and having taken two as instructed I ascended to my room and sank into an armchair. Four hours later I awoke. The sickness and piercing headache had gone and only my stomach was complaining – I needed some food. The following morning I left Chicago, my shaken self-assurance quite restored. My sudden illness was soon forgotten, except for a vow that I would never touch a malt drink again.

* * *

My experience in Chicago was the first in an increasingly frequent series of 'turns', as they rather quaintly came to be called. Sometimes the timing and nature of these turns was distinctly awkward: once, I regained consciousness to find myself in the flat in which I stayed, lying on my back and staring blankly at the ceiling. I had no idea how I got there. Some months after returning from my U.S. trip these turns, although different in nature and severity, were happening every fortnight. Instead of seeing a doctor, I concluded I must have inherited from my mother a tendency to suffer from migraine. This conclusion was, however, shattered when I made a discovery in a very casual way. As a visitor to Canada, I had to have a routine medical examination. It was to take only ten minutes. The doctor asked a few questions, then took my blood pressure. He knitted his brows and tried again. He faced me squarely: 'Have you been drinking lately?'

The year 1966 was drawing to a close. It was the New Year season, and I was a Scotsman, so I suppose there was some justification for his question. I assured him that I did not indulge except on rare occasions, and then only in moderation.

'Then you'd better see a doctor immediately,' he said, 'and make it a good one. I am not allowed to make any further examination. Next, please.'

There was a sense of foreboding as I waited for the appointment with my local doctor. During that week, I borrowed a book on high blood pressure from the library. The contents were divided into two sections – curable and incurable. In the latter section I read, 'The end of this disease is invariably tragic. The person may live for a few years after onset, but eventually succumbs to one of a number of vascular diseases, e.g. cerebral haemorrhage or coronary thrombosis.' I did not sleep well that night.

Afterwards, I learned that my trouble was known as 'malignant hypertension'. Needless to say, 'malignant' was used in a purely technical sense without any implication of malice or cunning, but the name seems to me quite apt. Malignantly it had stalked me over the previous months: just as a cat plays with a mouse it would catch me only to let me go again, leaving me nervous and anxious as to when I would next feel its grip. Malignantly it had finally pounced and pinned me down as 1966 moved on into 1967 – at a time of joy and happiness when we look forward to the future, making our resolutions and articulating our hopes. At 28, was I really trapped?

As a minister to the small Free Presbyterian congregation in Winnipeg, I preached about a God who had the whole of creation under his care. A sparrow did not fall to the ground without him. I could open my Bible and read a passage like this, from Isaiah:

> Why do you say, O Jacob, and speak, O Israel: 'My way is hidden from the LORD, and my just claim is passed over by my God'? Have you not known? Have you not heard? The everlasting God, the LORD, the Creator of the ends of the earth, neither faints nor is weary. There is no searching of his understanding. He gives power to the weak, and to those who have no might he increases strength. Even the youths shall faint and be weary, and the young men shall utterly fall, but those who wait on the LORD shall renew their strength; they shall mount up with wings like eagles, they shall run and not be weary, they shall walk and not faint (*Isa.* 40:27–31).

But what if death did come? I had continually reminded my congregation that even though we may pass through the valley of the shadow of death, if we can say, 'The Lord is my shepherd', we need fear no evil. I had done this for an eighty-year-old man who lived alone in a senior citizens' home. I had done it for a lady of forty-five years whose strength slowly ebbed away because of cancer. Now, as I lay in bed at night, I realized that these words were for me, too.

I wanted to know from the doctor how bad my condition was, and what the consequences might be. At that first appointment, the doctor practically dismissed my illness. He did, however, ask me to come back again in a week. I decided to cut the knot of uncertainty by trying my own pressure if I got the opportunity. I was visiting in the hospital one day and asked one of the staff if I could have the use of a blood-pressure machine. She gave me one, and a room to myself. (I had used one of these machines before, though this was the first time that I was taking my own blood pressure.) Having mastered the technique with some difficulty, I found that the reading was exceptionally high.

A doctor who was around at the time checked the reading and confirmed it. He took me downstairs and spent five minutes peering into my eyes with an ophthalmoscope. Eventually he laid it aside.

'You need medical attention at once', he said. I told him of the other appointment in a few days.

'Don't wait for that', he said, picking up the phone. In a few moments it was arranged that I be admitted to hospital the next day.

* * *

Dr Cuddy, under whose care I came into hospital, was a young man. He held the position of chief cardiologist in the Winnipeg General Hospital. He seemed quietly efficient as he took the pressure, first on one of my arms, then on the other. I was admitted to a two-bed ward. If I had felt really ill, I suppose I would have been glad to get some place where I could lay down my head in peace. As it was, having got over one of my turns directly before coming into hospital, I felt quite well. I was ready to enjoy the company, the attention, I might almost say the luxury, of hospital life.

Directly before coming into hospital, I had been living in the YMCA. Now, instead of the regular hunt for a suitable café in the evenings, meals were brought to my bedside.

Though the YMCA had little distinctively Christian about it, there was one feature for which I was thankful at the time. At the entrance was a board carrying a text which was changed every so often. One text which I was grateful they left unchanged for quite some time was, 'He who is faithful in what is least is faithful also in much.' Faithfulness: it seemed such a plodding virtue.

Canadians are absolutely in love with action. 'If you want action, drink 7-Up,' the hoardings screamed at you, while a passing bus issued the challenge, 'Go where you'll get action – join Canadian Enterprises.'

To compare faithfulness with action is rather like comparing the cart-horse, his head drooping to the ground, with the race-horse as he cleaves the air at a fast gallop. Yet faithfulness to my position was the only course of action open to me.

The tests I had were many and various. Some were quite simple, like the one where an injection was given to find out if I were suffering from excess secretion of a hormone which causes raised blood pressure. There was no alteration in the level produced, so this possibility was eliminated directly. Some were complicated, like the one where my kidney function was examined using a radioactive tracer.

One test in particular I found quite fascinating, since I was able to follow it on an internal television network. The lights were dimmed, heightening the atmosphere, and the eye of a TV screen showing an X-ray of the aorta, the main artery from the heart with its two branches, glowed eerily in the darkness. The picture, apparently suspended in mid-air, was so entirely detached from me as I lay on the table that I had to remind myself forcibly that it was part of my own internal anatomy I saw before me.

The object of the test was to insert a tube low down in one of the branches and feed it up into the aorta until it was opposite the two arteries which supplied the kidneys. On the edge of the screen I saw the tube snaking upwards. Since I had a local anaesthetic, I felt nothing. Onward it went until the end stopped opposite the renal arteries. Dye was pumped into the tube and suddenly, there were the two kidneys, their networks of blood vessels flared out as though the map of two miniature Amazons with all their branching tributaries had suddenly been stamped on the screen. I felt a burning sensation which built up to a climax and then rapidly passed away. X-ray photographs were taken. In a moment all was over. Lights were switched on again and I was wheeled off to make room for the next patient.

Gradually it became evident that the tests were all centring on the kidneys. I asked Dr Cuddy:

'Do I have a kidney disease?'

'Almost certainly,' he answered. 'This is what has caused your raised blood pressure.'

'Are both kidneys affected?' I asked.

'They probably are,' he told me.

This was the question which had preyed on my mind ever since I had read a text-book on the subject. It seemed from this that I fell into the incurable class. I was anxious in case just a few kind words would be said and that, with this verbal pat on the back, I would be turned out to await the inevitable. I confessed to having read the article on my condition.

'That was true ten years ago,' he told me. 'Since then various drugs have been developed which can control blood pressure.' I breathed a sigh of relief. After all, the kidney disease caused me no immediate discomfort, and after the pressure was controlled I expected to be rid of my sickness and headache. For the time being, I was put on guanethidine, one of the newer drugs for controlling blood pressure. I had a day or two of feeling rather dizzy while my body adjusted, but otherwise I felt none the worse.

An unspoken bond develops between the patient and the medical staff. Where mutual respect and confidence develop, a bond like this can form a chrysalis in which the patient's spirit, wounded and vulnerable through his illness, may grow and become strong until he is ready to take flight for himself. In any case, the chrysalis must break and be left behind, an empty shell. Thus I found it now.

I just had to walk with my own feet out of the ward, push open the swing-doors with my own hands, press for the elevator with my own finger and say 'Good morning' on my own account to whoever happened to be there before me.

9

The Homecoming

After being released from hospital, I decided to return home. Dr Cuddy told me I should wait three months at any rate before resuming work, and I thought this time could be spent as well in Scotland as anywhere else. It only remained for me to gather my few belongings, say goodbye to my friends, and in six hours the plane would carry me back to my own people once again.

To speak of saying 'goodbye' to my friends may seem final. Yet goodbye means literally 'God be with you', and I am sure that this was our genuine wish for each other. They did not forget me when I left, as I did not forget them. Such bonds are not severed by distance.

I suppose I expected that coming back to Scotland, as I did in February 1967, would be like fitting on an old glove. It was and it wasn't. I had left behind things like the garish neon signs, the overhead electric wires and the need to convert dollars to pounds. The Scottish accent which was a luxury commodity in Canada – I used to go up to the book department in the Hudson's Bay Stores just to hear a certain counter-clerk from Airdrie speak – now flowed freely around me. On the other hand, I had forgotten what congestion was like. In Manitoba, one million people had room to spill over into an area four times the size of Britain. Now distances seemed so short. In half-an-hour's flight from Glasgow I had reached Inverness, and a further half-hour by car took me to Dingwall and home.

Almost immediately after my arrival home, it was arranged that I go into hospital in Aberdeen. I did not take kindly to this at first. Aberdeen Royal Infirmary is a fine-looking building, but I was still at the withdrawal stage in relation to leaving Canada, and was seeing things through the eyes of one who had been adopted into the New World. I was ready to be critical of things British.

In Canada medicine was not some kind of sacred soil on which none but the initiated dare tread. I myself had been allowed to take my own blood pressure. (When I told this later to two general practitioners in the UK, they merely looked at each other with the same dismay with which two aged matrons discuss the indiscretions of the younger generation.)

The contrast between Canada and Britain was brought to a sharp focus in the ward round. If one saw the consultant in Canada, as often as not he was by himself. The conversation might be as follows:

> Things going all right? No ill-effects from the drugs we're giving you? No? Don't get up just now. I'll leave you to finish your dinner. Must rush off to have my own. You're doing fine.

How different the solemn progress of the ward-round in Britain! Slowly, with echoes of ancient councils, it moved down the ward from bed to bed. The consultant, though he walked with others, seemed to dwell in an invisible sanctum. The life of the council either radiated from him, or homed in upon him or pirouetted around him as its centre. Charts were detached from bed-ends and submitted to him for inspection. Occasionally at a word from him, one of the minions would detach herself from the group and scurry off up the ward in search of additional information, or some instrument to carry out further investigation. There would be whisperings and noddings and significant glances. Perhaps for a moment the grave visage of one of the medical team would relax to ask a question of the patient. Then the circle of the conclave closed again. More whisperings, more glances and final noddings all round before the chief put one foot forward towards the next bed signifying, 'Court adjourned.'

Towards the end of my stay, much to the envy of my fellow patients, I was given the freedom of Aberdeen and Aberdeenshire between mealtimes.

In solitude I explored St Machar's Cathedral. Solitude was just right for such an atmosphere. The light banter of conversation would have held one too much in the present. It needed solitude to allow oneself to be carried back into the past: to the time when the cathedral was the centre of Old Aberdeen, itself a self-contained unit, far from the bustle of the Torry docks or the easy-going rural atmosphere of Cults. The cathedral must have had its own kind of bustle, especially around the time of the Reformation, when the building changed hands. Walking along the aisles, I could hear these voices from the past.

Another day spent in solitude was quite different. I went up one side of the Dee Valley by bus to Banchory. House-wives were lost in earnest conversation; school children, bubbling over after the close of lessons, filled the air with their noise. This was life in the present and I sat on the periphery, a mere spectator. All the majesty of the mountains outside the window could not make me forget this.

While awaiting a bus to take me home, I sat in a café sipping tea. Once again I was in the midst of life but not part of it. I took a notebook out of my pocket and began a letter to a friend in Canada, attempting to establish some human contact for myself on the other side of the Atlantic. The exercise was inevitably one-sided, but sufficiently absorbing to make me forget myself until I noticed the waitress tidying up, as if to indicate that a café was hardly the place for letter composition. I was quite glad to return to the ward that night.

I was just becoming settled on a new drug when, one Sunday morning, I threw things rather out of kilter by giving an abnormally high reading of blood pressure. This quite mystified them at first, but I knew the secret myself all the time. I had been asked to take the F. P. service in Aberdeen that morning and had not wished to concern anyone around the hospital unnecessarily about this.

I decided to speak on a theme perhaps suggested by the surroundings. It was the 'Most High God' of Psalm 78. There, in the midst of preoccupation with so many mundane affairs, the voice of Wisdom seemed to call down to me, speaking of life to be sought and found on a plane so much higher than the plane of food and drink and what we should wear.

Early that Sunday morning I awoke and was ready to turn over again when I remembered, 'the sermon!' Had I clarified this point sufficiently in my mind? Was I ready to apply that other point? I lay awake churning these things over, and by the curious sympathy that exists between mind and matter, soul and body, by the time I was due to have my blood pressure taken, the state of my inner feelings registered on the mercury scale. (I heard afterwards that a friend in Canada to whom I related this incident told Dr Cuddy. His laconic remark was, 'Well, it wouldn't have been much of a sermon if his pressure hadn't risen!')

I remember we used to feel rather disappointed when we asked our father for an account of his experiences in the First World War. We wanted to share in the excitement of great campaigns and hear of the tactical brilliance of a general winning the day for his troops by an unexpected manoeuvre as the issue still hung in the balance. He didn't tell us any of this.

He gave us mere snapshots of his experiences; like the dream he had in a trench when up to his ankles in freezing mud, of being back home in Raasay warming his feet at the fire while his sister dried his socks; or how, when passing through a town, the bedraggled line of infantry squared their shoulders at the sound of the pipes, swelled out their chests and brought some semblance of rhythm to their steps. They would wave to the scattering of locals who had turned out to see them; for a time they felt proud to be British. Beyond the town, the tune of the pipes ended abruptly and the unmusical tramp began again. So it is with my memory of contacts in hospital. These are not graded in my mind according to their medical importance, even if for no better reason than that I did not know what was going on behind the scenes.

There is the memory of looking down one Sunday morning on the square in front of the ward where the helicopter landed which flew in patients from outlying parts. This time there was no helicopter. There was a ring of uniformed men from the Salvation Army, their caps off and their heads bowed in prayer.

We were two storeys above them, and even if there had been some likelihood of hearing what the man who led in prayer was saying, the wind which gusted across the courtyard carried very little up to us. Yet there was something symbolic. The normal sounds of the ward were hushed and we stood there, staff and patients, in silent acknowledgement of the God of healing.

One of the main tests was a biopsy in which a little piece of kidney tissue was cut out for examination. This was carried out by Dr MacLeod, the head of the Renal Unit in the Infirmary. After I came out of hospital, I went to see him with my brother James in the medical school where Dr MacLeod carried out his research. He invited us to sit down, and asked me what I intended to do.

My mind was still on Winnipeg, and I told him so. Abruptly he dismissed this. I was disappointed, even offended. My interests were still very much bound up with the con-gregation over there. From this side of the Atlantic such interest might seem microscopic. To me, they still seemed large. I did not realize he adopted this attitude from an understanding of the disease I was harbouring.

I was assured I could carry on preaching, but it would be advisable to be near a major medical centre. James suggested Edinburgh, and Dr MacLeod agreed that this would be suitable. I felt happy with this arrangement myself. I had spent my student days in Edinburgh, and was therefore quite familiar with the city. I left Aberdeen soon afterwards.

10

Clipped Wings

Freed for the first time in three months from hospital routine, I was eager to spread my wings. For this reason alone, I welcomed an invitation to the spring communion in Breasclete on the west coast of Lewis. Since my family had spent seven years in Stornoway, capital of the Outer Hebrides, in Canada I had often 'in dreams beheld the Hebrides'.

Breasclete lies on a beautiful west coast inlet. After driving across the brown moor of the central part of the island one welcomes all the more this strip of water surrounded by green. On the other side lie the hills of Bernera and beyond that again the mountains of Uig. It was the first time for years that I had come into contact with the close-knit village community characteristic of rural Lewis.

Years before, soon after I first came to Lewis as a boy of fourteen, I had gone out from Stornoway to Breasclete with a friend to catch rabbits. We went to a house where one of his relatives stayed, and I was struck by the easy, informal way in which neighbours came in and out. They entered unannounced, would sit for a time listening to the conversation and then leave with as little ceremony as when they arrived. Life was close to nature. Water was carried from a well in two pails slung from the shoulders. Fuel in the form of peat was dug from the ground. Corn was grown in long strips of land that ran down from the house.

We did not catch any rabbits, but I really wonder if my friend had set out with any great resolve in this direction. It seemed that discussion about family affairs, about the relative merits of different methods of catching wildlife, about the state of the crops that year, news from the town, etc., were just as important as going home with a full bag.

Many memories clustered around the little church in Breasclete. I could still see Coinneach Beag (Little Kenneth), the senior elder, walk down the aisle during the first singing. The slow, plaintive rhythm of the Gaelic singing exactly matched his tread. Every step bespoke gravity and his white hair, which spilled out from under a little black skull-cap, made him look like one of the ancient patriarchs. It was there that I had preached one of my first sermons, and there couldn't have been a better place. I was full enough of ideas, but clumsy in expression, and only able to stand a fleeting glimpse of the congregation now and then before lowering my eyes to the bookstand. However, a young preacher could not have had a more sympathetic audience.

I knew I could relax in such surroundings. There would be none of the strict hospital routine. I would not meet the new day with a sudden jolt at six in the morning as steel basins clattered and medicine trolleys rattled. Passage from night to day in Lewis was a gentle affair, helped on by a cup of tea.

But I am writing all this from memories of years back. I was never to reach Breasclete this particular time. I flew over to Stornoway and settled in at the manse, intending to take the bus the next morning. There was a mid-week service in the F. P. Church in Stornoway that night, and I could not but feel a rising tide of emotion as I sat down in the church where my father had been minister from 1952 to 1960.

So many elements intermingled, it would be fruitless to try and describe them. It made me bow my head in thanks. Was it for memories of the past, for all that had happened since I left the island, for being taken through my illness thus far, for the opportunity to return? As well ask Samuel when he set up a stone and called it 'Ebenezer', saying, 'Thus far the Lord has helped us.' It was for all these things, but I didn't stop to separate the strands.

After the service, the rest of the evening was spent in the company of friends who had been in Canada for many years. Time flew past, and it was late before we returned to the Stornoway manse. I felt elated. The sense of exile, which must ever follow anyone who leaves home surroundings, had slipped away from my shoulders.

Next morning, however, I awoke to a throbbing pain in the side of my head. The last time I had felt it was before going into hospital in Winnipeg. It didn't take long to realize it would be folly to think of carrying on to Breasclete. The doctor came in and gave me a few tablets. Before long I was well enough to return by plane to Inverness.

Chronic illness has a tendency to break one down. One feels like a satellite gone out of orbit, forced to drift off through regions quite without meaning in terms of one's cherished ambitions. It had been like this in the café in Banchory. What was I doing there sipping tea while the rest of the world was working? It was because of my illness, pure and simple. As I lay in bed after returning home, thoughts such as these revolved through my mind. I had been forcibly taken from the Canadian setting. In a sense, this illness that took me home had set me free from responsibility. Yet I was not my own master. Each time I tried to assert my freedom, an invisible leash pulled me to heel.

It was while thoughts like these simmered in my mind that I idly picked up a paperback copy of Kierkegaard's Edifying Discourses. I lighted on one discourse, entitled 'The Enthusiast'. Kierkegaard describes a man with an 'idée fixe'. Others might describe it as a 'bee in the bonnet'. Against appearances he works for its realization. He meets with disappointments, but his spirit is undaunted. Slowly his dreams begin to bear fruit. The Danish philosopher had struck a chord.

I had needed the commitment of 'The Enthusiast' to face the situation in Winnipeg. I had worked on, confident that fruit would appear. But that had all come to an abrupt conclusion when I had landed in hospital. Now I had my illness to contend with. But could not enthusiasm surmount illness too? Nature abhors a vacuum. I wished to have a cause to relate to, and then this vacuum of empty days and nights would fill with plans and interests, and life would assume a pattern once again.

(On reflection, I realize that the prevailing sin of the invalid is discontent. I had dressed up my discontent in the form of a virtue, the virtue of zealous enthusiasm which, conscious of the call of God, will brook no hindrance. But I was not really asking, 'Lord, what do you want me to do?' I was taking the restless impulse of my own spirit as sufficient warrant for going ahead. I did not really believe that 'they also serve who only stand and wait'.)

A Presbytery meeting was due shortly and I was asked to appear. To everyone's surprise, I said I did not wish to commit myself to staying at home at present. I wished to leave my way open to return to Canada. For the time being, the matter was shelved. I phoned the Canadian immigration authorities in Glasgow to see if I would be accepted. I was told I would have a fifty-fifty chance.

As it turned out, I did not need to test which fifty I fell into. Some time after, I was phoning the Convener of the Dominions and Overseas Committee of my denomination. I was told a deputy had just been appointed to go to Winnipeg for six months. My services would not be required.

Amy Carmichael tells a charming story in one of her books. As a child, she asked God to change the colour of her eyes one night, and next morning eagerly rushed to the mirror. Her eyes were still the same.

'I did not lose my faith in God,' she says. 'I still believed he answers prayer. Only, sometimes he says, 'No!'" In the light of future events, I would add that the timing of this particular 'No!' which I received was very clearly from God.

* * *

Two visits stand out, from that summer of 1967. One was to Kames, in the Kyles of Bute, where I was born and brought up. In my memory it remained a cameo of rocks and heather and shore-line along which, as though incidentally, were strung houses for human habitation. Nature, not mankind, was omnipresent. One weekend, I arrived to take the services in the little church where my father had preached for over twenty-one years.

On Saturday the lure of the surroundings, with all their memories, drew me out irresistibly for a walk. I went down the brae to the shore (why did distances seem so much shorter now?) and then along to the end of the village to the tank-landing. This was a massive concrete area where tanks landed during the war in practice for the invasion of the

Continent in 1944. I stood for a time, thankful to let nature preach in silence. I looked up at the hill behind me and thought how much better the view would be from the top. It seemed it could be climbed with ease. Forestry trees, planted since my boyhood days, were thinly spaced and left plenty of room to pass between them.

I began the ascent vigorously, but soon had to slacken the pace, and it took all the inducement of the expanding beauty of the surroundings to make me keep on. The smaller hills, like the Douhin in Tighnabruaich which dominated the skyline at sea-level, were beginning to dip slowly downwards until they seemed as no more than an outcrop of rock at the base of the higher hills beyond.

Still, I could not deceive myself. Every few steps, my muscles became as taut and inelastic as a leathern thong. I would throw myself to the ground and hear the pounding of my pulse, which seemed to beat the earth below me. There was the possibility of turning back, but the effort of battling through scrub and trailing strands of heather even on a downward slope was as uninviting as continuing the now relatively short distance to the top. In a short time I was able to cut diagonally across the hillside. But by now my inner vision had changed so that the attractive dun colour of the hills had become merely drab brown, and I thought more of the chill of the wind than of the pattern it made as it raced over the sea below me.

In retrospect, it was foolhardy to have undertaken a walk like this. The reason I did was that I considered I should be improving. If time were the great healer (and I thought then that time and rest under the treatment regimen for high blood pressure were all I really needed) I should now be practically normal. What I did not realize was that the disease, like a harpoon plunged into a whale, never surrendered an inch. If I lay quiet, I might not feel it. The moment I exerted myself, however, my illness became evident, and every effort under these circumstances, instead of enabling me to release myself, only gave it the opportunity to move one step nearer the inevitable end.

Another visit I made at this time was to Raasay, a long strip of an island sandwiched between the towering Red Hills of Skye and the equally imposing mountains of Applecross. An aunt of mine had once been schoolmistress on Fladda, one of the islands off the north end of Raasay. Now Fladda was empty. Another aunt had served in the school to the south of Raasay. My grandfather had stayed with her and often walked the nine miles to Torran at the north end, to take services. Since there would soon be only one family left in Torran, I was keen to hold a service there. Perhaps it might be the last.

Ruaraidh MacLeod, with whom I was staying, strongly urged me against it. We could have a car for six miles, he reminded me, but there were still three miles to walk. His arguments fell on deaf ears. I looked on the journey as a kind of pilgrimage enshrined in family memory. To the pilgrim, obstacles simply present a challenge to be surmounted.

Ruaraidh had been brought up at the north end of the island and would have been glad to return, but he was crippled with arthritis and would not think of undertaking the journey. I carried on with arrangements. The car came. It was a wonderful, sunny day. Just as we were leaving, the door of the house opened and Ruaraidh came stiffly down the path clutching his stick.

'I'm coming with you,' he said.

No comments were passed, but when I think back, it rather makes me smile. An expedition mounted to the north end of Raasay to hold a final service. One minister, his

Family group, Tighnabruaich, 1951:
    Back row- Fraser, Rev. James Tallach, Elizabeth Tallach, Andrew;
    Front row- John, James, Cameron.

Fraser in Canada, 1965.

Fraser and Mother

Fraser, John and James

internal chemistry all awry. One elder, his movement severely hampered by arthritis. The weather seemed to buoy up our spirits marvellously. We reached the end of the road and took to the hills.

'I'm all right when I get going,' said Ruaraidh as he painfully eased himself out of the car. For a moment he steadied himself, then he hardly stopped until the three miles were completed. At times he even forgot the need for a stick as he lifted it to point out places connected with his boyhood.

The boys of the family lingered about the door when the time of the service came, and I remembered my own hesitation in childhood before entering the shadows of a church on a beautiful day. Yet the little group were soon quiet and attentive, as we looked beyond the passing beauty of a summer's day; beyond the ceaseless ebb and flow of life itself, to the bedrock, 'I am who I am.'

* * *

Having roamed here and there during the summer, I eventually faced up to the decision, made earlier, that I should settle in Edinburgh. The first problem was accommodation. The 1967 Festival was in full swing and, if anyone doubted it, he needed only to try to find a place to stay. I searched through many advertisements for accommodation and at first one place seemed promising. I began to have misgivings, however, soon after arriving at the address.

We were on the ground floor and I expected we would go up. Instead the landlady took me down, and down. We entered a dark hallway in the basement. She opened a door and I stepped inside. The bed, the wardrobe and the chair in this small room seemed to be set amidst a heavy gloom. I looked up at the window. Facing it was a grey concrete wall, and above the level of the wall was a thin slit of light in which the clouds raced past with enviable freedom. I could not live in this perpetual twilight.

I tried to think of anyone connected with the Free Presbyterian Church in Edinburgh who kept students. One house I remembered might be able to keep me, but only until the students returned. Once again, as had so often happened before, I drew a blank. I was just going out the door when the lady of the house picked up the phone and dialled a number. A short conversation ensued and the phone was replaced. 'I've just been speaking to Effie,' she reported, 'and she says to bring up your bags right away.'

Effie came from Skye, and though she had long since emigrated to the Lowlands, her spirit of Highland hospitality had never left her. She might well have excused herself a burden so suddenly thrust upon her. She had a house and a husband to look after and, besides her work at home, she was matron of a home which cared for mental patients.

I had hardly arrived when I took one of my turns. I had been asked to take a mid-week service. This should have caused me little trepidation. The address would be a short one. Why I should have been so apprehensive is difficult to say. I only know I was, and next morning I paid the price in the usual way.

I expected to get over it quite quickly in the same way as a child, having once seen a wave sweep up a beach, can predict the point which the next wave will reach and the time it will take to recede. I had the measure of my illness now, and could live with it. This time, however, the wave rolled on. After two days, although I was on my feet, I was still very shaky and feeling thoroughly ill.

There was a peculiar tingling in my muscles as though, under the smooth surface of my skin, a war were being waged on a microscopic level. I looked for a hand to steady me. A GP had been in already, and had told me there was nothing he could do, except give me pills to control the vomiting. Two days later came the turning-point and, with it, relief.

In looking back now, I can see that renal failure was approaching steadily. The attacks were becoming more severe and I was recovering from them more slowly. Between the attacks I felt quite well, but all the time my limits of performance were being steadily narrowed down. I was becoming more and more anaemic, and though in sitting or walking this did not show itself, any little exertion drained me of strength.

11

No Fixed Abode

I passed that winter and the following spring in Edinburgh. Then, in the early summer of 1968, I went down to London to preach for a minister who (ironically) was on deputation work in Canada. I took the opportunity of visiting one or two places of interest.

'This, ladies and gentlemen, is the Tower. That is the room where Raleigh was imprisoned. This is the gate where prisoners were led out to execution,' etc. It was impossible to shut out the real life around me; it was a life of buses and trains and people, all intent on getting somewhere on time. But something was dying within me.

For two weeks I stayed in a flat overlooking Battersea Park. My Aunt Katy had come down to keep house for me. She had been in London for years as matron of an Aged Pilgrims' Home. One day I drove her to Hornsey Rise for a tea in her honour. The driving was hectic. Unused to the city, I was perpetually getting into the wrong lane, having to take a detour and then seek out the original route. Eventually we arrived at what to me, in the circumstances, was indeed a Home of Rest. We were shown round the establishment and then came the tea. When we returned, I logged up the number of hours I had been driving and found it came to four and a half. Thankfully I dropped off to sleep.

Next morning as I awoke, the old queasy feeling was back again. I got up and vomited. This time, there was blood. I realised that, as far as work was concerned, my stay in London was over. My aunt phoned the doctor. He took a long time coming and we soon realised why. We were staying at 12a Prince of Wales Mansions and he had gone to number 12, the one below. When he didn't find us there, he had gone right down the whole row of houses before coming back to have another try. It said much for him that he didn't just give up, but I felt that whatever his store of patience, it would be tactful to use the greatest economy of words possible when he arrived.

'What's wrong?' he asked as he mopped his brow.

'I put up a cupful of blood,' I explained.

'St Thomas' Hospital,' was all he said. He filled in a white form which was to be my introduction and was gone.

A short time in the ambulance, and I was back in the old familiar surroundings again. I was becoming accustomed to the routine. The crisp, clean sheets, the faint medical smell, the clip of heels along the corridor, even the clatter of a steel basin falling from its stand spoke the language I was beginning to understand. The clockwork efficiency of the staff gave the perfect surroundings in which one could regain health and strength.

There is, of course, the other side. When the end is not restoration to health, the external order only provided a stark contrast to the break-up within one's self. For the time being, however, I did not think such negative thoughts. I could feel that, as I emerged to consciousness each morning, the day before me would prove more pleasant than the previous. I would be able to walk a further distance down the ward without the onset of dizziness; I would have a better appetite for food; my spirits would improve.

A number of persons stand out in my memory. My first companion was a man from Turkey. He was small and wizened and had his eyes bandaged after some operation. Propped up on pillows, he faced blankly into the middle of the ward. I wanted to be friendly to this involuntary outcast from the society around him. Where did he come from? How long had he been in London? The conversation flowed freely enough. We came round to the church. I couldn't see his eyes but I imagine that, behind the bandages, they became secretive and withdrawn at that point. Confidentially he leaned over to me.

'I'll tell you the truth about them,' he said. 'They're all secret societies – like the Freemasons.' Rather foolishly I met this head-on. For the next half-hour or so I found that, small and wizened and blind-folded though he might be, he could wield his cudgels in defence of an argument with great spirit. I am sure the row of sleeping forms on the beds opposite were more alive than they seemed and were enjoying the entertainment. It was I who came out of the encounter bruised and bleeding.

The personalities of the nurses differed immensely. One would work as though spurred on by some inspiration from Florence Nightingale herself. There was no let-up. Her smile was genuine, but it was also a matter of duty. Any tendency to yawn or to day-dream was immediately suppressed. By contrast, another worked as though she were a kind-hearted person just in from the street who had found a number of people in need. She would chat and listen to the various complaints and all the time, as though by way of a side-line, she would be straightening bed-clothes, tidying the locker, taking temperatures and checking charts.

That summer was extremely hot. Fortunately, the ward had a balcony at the front where one could sit catching the few breezes that blew, and watching the barges ply up and down the Thames. On the other side of the river were the Houses of Parliament and Big Ben, whose chimes were silenced during the day with the noise of the surrounding traffic, but which dominated the night time. The huge illuminated face looked in the windows like a giant moon, while the chimes boomed across the river.

The ward round might linger long over some beds, but I was usually treated to no more than a casual remark, and the train of medics passing my bed hardly paused. Of course, as in Edinburgh, there was nothing that could be done. My kidneys had been further damaged, and the part damaged could not be repaired. One thing that might have warned me was a card I got from the sister just before I left. It told my blood group, and was to be produced if ever I needed an emergency transfusion. Throughout this time, I did not lack for visitors. My youngest brother John came down to hold the services instead of me. Friends visited regularly. The week in hospital passed quickly and soon it was time to go.

Rarely have I felt so acutely the symptoms of withdrawal from hospital care. I was back again looking out over Battersea Park at the joggers going round in a seemingly endless circle, expending much effort only to arrive back where they came from. There was no progression, no goal. I felt I could identify with them. There was the loneliness of this treadmill of effort. For the moment the hospital had given me a clear identity. There had been a clearly-defined goal: to get better. Now I was better again, and being so, should have my office, my house, my sphere of effort. I had none of these.

How good at a time like this to think of the one without reputation, without home, who wandered around the cities of Palestine! Yet for him there was nothing of the bewilderment, the ennui, the self-pity that afflicted me. He knew his mission. His home was beyond this world. I could not lay claim to the same spirit as he had. Yet he had bound up persons like me. He was the shepherd, I the sheep. And having the heart of a shepherd, he was 'touched with the feeling of my infirmities'.

These thoughts were interrupted by the phone. I had been asked to take the services of the communion season at the F. P. Church in North Uist. Would I still be able to come? I said that I would. Shortly afterwards I would be preaching at another communion season in Bonar, in Sutherland. I was moving around without any centre, but nothing can help to drive home the truths of the gospel like preaching it. Soon I was on the night train back to Scotland, and into harness once again.

From the air, North Uist looks like a pattern of lochs interlaced by strips of land. It seems either to be just emerging from the Atlantic breakers, or to be just sinking beneath them. When one lands, this appearance is forgotten. The lochs are hidden in hollows, and it is the ridges of land that stand out on the horizon. Within a short time, I had both views. I arrived by plane at Benbecula, which is joined to North Uist by a causeway, and in a short time was speeding to the manse by car.

Although life on the island is normally lived at a leisurely pace, in a sense the pace quickens at communion time. That Wednesday I had a service in a small meeting-house on the moors. Next morning there was a service in the main church; in the evening, another on the other side of the island. So it went on until the communion service proper on Sunday morning. On Monday there was the final thanksgiving service before dispersal.

After London, the soft limpid air of the Outer Hebrides, the wide sweeping beaches, the boundless sea, were a relaxation in contrast to the tensions of the city; but it was not with the landscape I had come to deal but people – people in their relationship with God. On Thursday night, I remember preaching on the passage in Zechariah telling of Joshua, the high priest, standing before God in filthy garments, awaiting a change of clothes from God himself. I preached, I suppose, convincingly enough. To be pleased with this alone, however, would be as reprehensible as for a man who lectured on the dreadful power of nuclear weapons to be satisfied with conveying a clear grasp of the facts. If the facts did not overawe his own spirit with the realization that he himself was under the shadow of a nuclear holocaust, then all his knowledge only went to increase his own condemnation. If I put others in the place of Joshua, then I must realizethat I, too, needed a change of clothes.

On Saturday, I was to preach the preparation sermon. However, I myself felt far from prepared at the time. I took as a text the prayer of the hundred and sixth Psalm, 'Remember me, O Lord, when you show favour to your people.' I found comfort in pointing out cases in the Bible where God reached out in grace to the unworthy, and found something of that peace which Christ says owes its origin to no earthly source – 'not as the world gives do I give to you' – but comes from God himself. I experienced once again the fact that God does not create a hunger he himself cannot satisfy.

In preaching, I felt I was far from the frame of mind which I would have liked. However, no doubt my illness played a part in this. I was in the last stages before renal failure; my blood count was probably less than half normal, and hence any extra exertion produced a feeling akin to the childhood nightmare where one strives with all one's might to run, only to find oneself held back by invisible hands. Hence, part of the difficulty I was meeting may well have arisen from my mental and physical condition. After speaking for a short time my mouth would become dry, and my words difficult to form.

I wrestled with the subject, but was always conscious that I was failing to reach the heart of it. My mind simply would not respond. Yet, the fact that in the end I did manage to preach was a further illustration of the fact that, as Psalm 103 tells us, 'He knows our frame (even in illness); he remembers that we are dust.'

My future sister-in-law, Ishbel, and her family from Skye were attending the communion and on Monday I went down through Benbecula to South Uist with them. For Ishbel's mother it was a sentimental journey, as she had previously taught there. I myself had never been beyond South Harris, though I had lived in Stornoway for seven years. We stopped for a picnic on a hillock. It was a world without sound. Out on the loch below us, a boat glided out from a hidden bay as though propelled by enchantment.

Curious to see where it came from, we ran down to the water's edge. Suddenly the experience of Kames repeated itself. My muscles stiffened, and I found I could hardly drag my feet. There was heather everywhere, and I had to return uphill. I had no wish to let the others know how I felt as it would have cut our time short. I walked up at an angle towards the road where I knew the going would be easier. When I reached the car I recovered quite quickly, but the narrow limits within which I was operating were driven home in no uncertain terms. I was about a week out of hospital, and had felt my discharge was equivalent to a passport to health. If love is blind through wishful thinking, hope is not far behind. Being discharged had brought plans, and plans needed health to carry them out. Unconsciously, I turned a blind eye to the recurring attacks I was suffering.

We continued our run in the car. We visited Lochmaddy, where I met a former school friend who was by then a minister in Benbecula. We went on to the very south of South Uist, where we had tea in a hotel. By evening we were back in the north again. What had happened by the loch became no more than an unpleasant interlude. I saw no reason to withdraw from the commitment to preach the next week in Bonar Bridge.

12

Love Is Strong as Death

At the Bonar Bridge communion, I stayed on a croft above the village. From the front door, hills and mountains swept away to the horizon. Swathes of corn rustled against the white washed walls.

The Saturday sermon fell to me, and a text kept recurring to my mind: 'Set me as a seal upon your heart, as a seal upon your arm' (*Song of Sol.* 8:6). I had intended to preach on this text before I had been taken into hospital. I suppose, like all texts from which one preaches with any measure of conviction, it had arisen out of my need at the time. 'Upon your heart' – that was an appeal for the love of another. 'Upon your arm' – that was an appeal for practical help based on that love. But it would not do simply to spill out one's own personal feelings. I had to transform my own feelings into a more general application to the Christian life, and ensure that my views did not clash with the context.

'For love is as strong as death.' I sat in the car in front of the house on Saturday morning, puzzling over this. To remain inside the house in such wonderful weather seemed a waste of precious sunshine. It streamed in the window and, in spite of a tendency (due to anaemia) to feel chilled very easily, I felt warm. Love and death. The two were poles apart. Love was like the sun, bringing to life delicate shades of colour unsuspected before. The dull, sombre hills suddenly burst out in a thousand different hues of green and brown. But death, like a cold, grey shroud, reduced variety to a dull uniformity.

Yet, though different from each other in nature, their power was alike. Death crept up silently, without questioning. There was a naked strength which met impassively all appeals for pity. So with love. Its power consisted, not in impressive speech, but in a depth of feeling that would brook no refusal. It found the reason why it must act, not in persuasive rhetoric, but simply in the fact that it existed, and it must gain the object of its desire.

The time came for the service, and suddenly I felt totally unfit. A great tiredness seemed to blanket me. I had hardly slept the night before. I began my subject wearily, but the subject itself took over, and weariness was soon forgotten.

Nevertheless, all this time death was calling me. Each time I had an indication of my poor physical condition, death called. He called in the breathlessness, in the way I shivered in an atmosphere warm enough for others, in recurrent nausea. I brushed him off. He never protested. But I did not realize that he remained in the background. Indeed he drew closer and closer. I had been exhausted in Uist by walking for half an hour on the moor. In Bonar, I was exhausted simply by walking round the end of the house through the long grass. Death did not insist and, foolishly, I took this to be evidence of weakness. But he could wait. He was strong.

After Saturday, I had only one more service on the Sunday evening. It was the ageless theme, emphasized time and again in Scripture: 'All flesh is grass, and all its loveliness is like the flower of the field. The grass withers, the flower fades ... but the word of our God stands for ever' (*Isa.* 40:8).

How ironic! I preached earnestly to others and yet, perhaps, if I had not spoken so loudly myself, I might have been silent and reflective enough to hear that this voice also called to me. I had hopes of settling down, hopes of a modicum of peace and security. I cannot remember any sense of foreboding for the future. Indeed, directly after the service, I felt the opposite.

After Bonar, there was a calm. I went down to Hilton, one of the fishing villages on the Moray Firth. The easy tenor of village life tended to reduce one's metabolism till it was barely ticking over. Had I been well, no place could have been more relaxing. I was free to do a thousand and one things, and yet found it difficult to set myself resolutely to any. Sometimes I took a walk. Yet, even in this, breathlessness came readily. The raised beach at the far end of the village was flat enough, but any movement from the grass to the sand brought trouble.

I tried to plough through a stretch of sand, and ended by sitting all in a heap, a pretty disgruntled heap at that. I looked out to sea, and saw the bombers from Lossiemouth droning over again and again, and the sudden white spouts from the Firth as their practice bombs landed. The seeming futility of the exercise matched my spirit. It was the café in Banchory situation again, only worse. I was not only disjointed: I was ill, and becoming more so. My sense of self-assurance was breaking down. One night I swung my legs over the edge of the bed and started when I realized how ghostly white they were. The next time I went into town, I got some iron pills from the doctor. Through it all, I managed to carry on a reasonably normal round of visiting and preaching.

Everyone was so kind, and yet there was a sense of isolation. A fishing village grows out of the sea, and its characters are strong and hardy as the rocks which take the full brunt of the ocean and toss it back again. I was told stories of heroism and daring. Mr MacKay next door had won a medal for life-saving. One did not give way to frailty; one battled against it and won.

I only knew now that I was retreating. As I sat on the sand-dune or on the edge of my bed, I was retreating; as I tried to exert my voice in preaching and felt a vice-grip tighten around my larynx, I was retreating. As I cradled my head in my hands with dizziness after a walk, or felt squeamishness after a meal, I knew that I was not really fighting any more. In fact, it was foolish to fight. Far better to sit in the shelter and watch while the seabirds fought with the wind and the boats battled through the waves.

I remember mentioning to some local people that I felt ill, and was worried. I could hardly blame them for telling me about a young man whom they knew who thought he was ill. He went to the doctor, and was told that it all lay in his imagination. Did they think that I was becoming neurotic? But the time was long past when I might have regarded my illness as a mere figment of my imagination.

After a fortnight in Hilton, I came to Dingwall at the beginning of September for the annual F. P. Church Conference. Dr Hugh Gillies, a friend from Stornoway, was staying with us. One afternoon, we went for a walk up by Tulloch Castle. Suddenly, our walk lost its relevance for me. An unmistakable feeling told me that I would not be attending the Conference. I would be laid out with a further bout of sickness.

The doctor came. I expected the usual treatment, and that in a short time I would be on my feet again. I heard and discussed news of the Conference at second-hand from my bed. Then came the phone-call. Who phoned, I cannot say. It did not matter anyway. I only knew that my mother's voice was strangely hesitant. She kept saying phrases like 'We hope so,' and 'Who can tell?' I knew instinctively that she was speaking about me, although she left the other person to do most of the talking, possibly out of awareness that I could overhear. Something was far wrong. Indeed, I knew now that I was unlikely to get better. What my internal chemistry had been telling me over the past few months was now verified by a laboratory technician, who had tested a blood sample which the doctor had previously taken.

Strangely, this voice from without hardly moved me at all. Possibly it was because the message was not accompanied by a crisis in my condition. I lay looking at the ceiling after the phone call and knew that I could hear and see and touch and breathe as easily as I could five minutes before. Something had registered, a message had been received, but that was all. It is curious how one's intellectual and one's emotional responses may be strangely out of phase with each other.

When my grandmother died in Dingwall in 1962, I mourned for her days before the actual event. I paid a visit to Strathy Point, in Caithness, after a period of watching her life gradually ebb away. Out on the moor the wind, the waves dashing on the hollow caves beneath my feet, the great expanse of waters, acted as a catalyst. Nature was untamed, impulsive, uninhibited, and in these surroundings I could give my feelings free expression. At the same time, there came a great crystallizing. Feelings of respect and affection gleaned from a thousand different experiences coalesced into one. I returned to the house in Dingwall with a calmness in my mind, as though the inevitable had already happened. On the day of the funeral, when I should have expected all the feelings of grief to reach a climax, I was strangely detached. I knew that there was a mighty truth in what took place before my eyes – 'dust to dust, ashes to ashes'. But I could not enter into that. Instead I idly read what was written on some of the stones. I believe I had something of the same experience after this phone call.

Some months previously in Edinburgh, before I ever thought that death might lie in the near future, as I was going out to preach, the words from Solomon's Song of Songs came to my mind: 'Rise up, my love, my fair one, and come away. For lo, the winter is past, the rain is over and gone. The flowers appear on the earth; the time of singing has come and the voice of the turtledove is heard in our land . . . Rise up, my love, my fair one, and come away!'

Winter was the present; death would bring Christ face to face. Death then became, simply, the call of Christ to deeper fellowship in a land where the glimpses of summer we may have here would be changed into permanent enjoyment. Of course, I did not argue it out this way. The experience came as a unified whole like the sudden appearance of a beautiful scene which stops one's breath in admiration. Before leaving the house, I retreated into my room again, partly so that I might linger over this experience and partly that I might regain mastery of my feelings.

Now was this phone call perhaps the human part of the divine 'Rise up'? Yet, beyond the tones of my mother's voice, I could discern no beckoning to higher worlds. No vista opened out before me. I thought only, 'When will the ambulance come? Will the stretcher-bearers be able to negotiate the stairs?' They did indeed manage and shortly I found myself twenty miles away – that was before the Kessock Bridge was built – in Raigmore Hospital, Inverness.

That is, Raigmore Hospital as it was, before being razed to the ground to make way for the present imposing edifice. It was a group of low-set buildings erected during the Second World War and still retaining the utility look of that period. I was shunted to and fro at first. I remember lying in one ward and watching a nurse counting out medicines while a man lay groaning in the bed beside me. Eventually I was placed in a side-room. I had only myself for company, and not very pleasant company at that. I was continually sick, a sickness that was not followed by any of the relief that active sickness might give.

I had taken a copy of Bunyan's *Pilgrim's Progress* with me into hospital. One day, when my brother James called, I asked him to read Bunyan's account of Christian's battle with Apollyon. As I lay there, fighting for breath, Bunyan's description seemed very real to me.

One symptom of my illness with which Raigmore dealt effectively was an irritating itch, which was worst along my back. This itch was associated with the high percentage of urea in my blood. Medically, of course, this was only of the most peripheral concern. The main trouble was kidney failure. I was required to drink large quantities of water, and this I doggedly set myself to do. Presumably, the aim was to force what capacity the kidneys had into maximum activity, but practically it was hopeless. By mid-afternoon, I would find the target I was set receding from view. I suppose it was like trying to force water into a saturated sponge.

Company was not welcome, apart from my own immediate relatives and the staff. I could, however, watch without direct involvement the man who used to take out the ashes from the furnace in the wing opposite. Daily he came and shook the ashes out into his barrow, and trundled off with them. That's life, I thought; that's life.

And yet, no-one had told me that I was going to die. The eyes of all the doctors I had seen up till now had looked into mine, and behind them was the knowledge that I was suffering from a fatal disease. Yet never once, to my memory, were the implications of my disease discussed with me.

True, on some unconscious level, my body told me, but this did not break into a clear, rational statement. From the medical standpoint, there was no dubiety. When admitted to Winnipeg General Hospital, my blood urea was 74 mg. At St Thomas' Hospital, the reading was 215 mg. Directly before admission to Raigmore, the level of blood urea was 406 mg.

After total renal failure, three months at the outside is the length of time that a patient can expect to live if he has no treatment. There was no treatment available in Raigmore. I might have been transferred to Aberdeen, but the places on kidney machines there were full. Day after day I drew nearer to the brink.

13

My Underworld

Should patients in such circumstances be told what their prospects are? Speaking for myself, I can only say that when I did learn at a much later stage how seriously ill I had been, I felt deep resentment. It was not that I could have acted as Socrates did, calmly disposing of his affairs, bringing death into focus, and producing philosophical gems to be forever cherished by his disciples. My feeling was more down to earth. Was this not my body which had become diseased? Indeed, was not the disease itself my own? No-one experienced its symptoms but myself, and certainly the consequences must be my own to face. Why then should everyone else be talking about them?

From a spiritual point of view it can be most salutary to know if one is facing the end. Tuberculosis used to be the scourge of the Highlands, yet it was called 'an galar bean-naichte' (the blessed disease). This did not arise from a cruel kind of black humour. Those who were smitten were left for many months, usually, while the illness progressed. They knew the inevitable end in those days before the development of streptomycin. There was time to reflect, often in little sheilings, where they were taken to enjoy the pure, fresh air. Not a few learned to pray the prayer of Hezekiah in his illness,

'O LORD, I am oppressed, undertake for me,' and went on to know his assurance, 'O LORD, you have cast all my sins behind your back.'

Whatever my own state of knowledge, the doctors spoke frankly to my relatives. Dr Knox, the consultant at Raigmore, took my mother out one day and sat with her on a bench in the grounds. I was not responding to treatment. They had no machines in Raigmore to take the place of the kidney. The nearest large medical centre to Inverness was at Aberdeen. There were kidney machines at Aberdeen, and I would normally be transferred there in an emergency; but the places in Aberdeen were all taken. I would have to stay in Raigmore. Need any more be said?

At the same time, I had a curious reaction which I was to notice a number of times in the future. When very ill I did not wish strange company, but neither could I bear to remain in the room by myself. I had to get out. I wanted to see other sights and feel plain, ordinary things, like a gust of wind on my face. Once, the desire to burst out of my confinement was so strong that I cajoled my brother into getting a wheelchair and wheeling me out along the corridor. When we passed open doors, I craned my neck to see all that I could. I wanted to pack as much experience as I could into the ten-minute run.

My brother James was working as a doctor at Bellshill Hospital at this time. He came north for a few days' holiday and, seeing my condition, determined that he would try to do something. I had been attending the Deaconess Hospital in Edinburgh, so James phoned to see if there was a bed available. There was.

In a sense, I could not have complained if I had been left in Raigmore to die. It happened to thousands of sufferers from kidney disease every year. The machines were not there for them, and funds not available to buy them. (In fact it was while James was working in Edinburgh Royal Infirmary, before commencing his medical course, that the first kidney machine had been tried in Scotland. This was a mere six years before. It was only since then that centres like Aberdeen, Edinburgh, and Glasgow had developed small units for chronic patients. The number of places available, however, was far below the demand.)

I can still remember the relief I felt when I heard that there was going to be some action. I had no clear idea what might happen if I stayed on in Raigmore, and we never discussed it. I thought that the blood transfusion which I was given might provide the magic solution. Instead, I was as sick after it as before. Now, at last, there was to be movement.

I was transferred by plane. The flight went without a hitch, apart from a delay at the Edinburgh end, waiting for an ambulance. I was back in the Deaconess Hospital again, this time right up on the top floor of the hospital among the octogenarians. There was a curious serenity; I felt quite calm and at ease.

The man in the bed beside me was complaining that sufficient attention had not been given to his case. A short figure appeared and walked silently past our beds. My companion recognized the medical consultant and began to call out, 'Doctor, doctor.' The doctor carried on into an office. Ten minutes later he emerged and made his way to my bed. He had some charts with him. It was now nearly midnight, and he spoke in a low voice.

The level of your blood urea is dangerously high. We cannot treat this here, in the Deaconess Hospital.

We will have to transfer you immediately to the
Royal Infirmary.

Once again there was the stretcher, the quiet intimacy of
the back of an ambulance, broken only by the droning of the
engine as we threaded our way through silent streets. There
was the screech of brakes, then silence; followed by the
wrenching open of steel doors, and voices. I was whisked
through corridors, one pair of folding doors, and then,
looking up, I saw two faces smiling down, aiming evidently to
reassure. The faces belonged to two nurses, who were
swathed up to the neck in blue cassocks. Their faces seemed
almost detached, swimming in the air.

From that point these nurses (from the Renal Isolation
Unit) took over. There was another pair of swing doors, and
with a few more deft manoeuvres of the trolley, I found myself
in a small room, almost no larger than myself. How I rejoiced
that, at last, inactivity had given way to action.

The smiling faces retreated. Another face, with a more
serious expression, appeared. This was Dr Lambie, one of the
consultants. She told me I was to be dialysed. This involved
pouring liquid into my abdominal cavity, leaving it there for
twenty minutes, and then withdrawing it.

One does not, of course, think of having a cavity in one's
abdomen. The layers of intestine leave no spaces. Nevertheless, like a balloon with all the air sucked out, there is a
potential cavity between the intestines and the outer wall.
Quite a large cavity it is, too, and it can take a surprising
volume of fluid.

In some cases, I was told, this worked: in others it did not.
They could only hope that in my case it would. Dr Lambie
left and the registrar, an Australian, began the actual dialysis.

He was a tall man with an easy, laconic manner. A tube was inserted through the mid-line of the abdominal wall and lowered till one felt a curious tingling in the back. The open end of this firm tube was then linked up with a length of flexible tubing, which draped from a large up-turned bottle, suspended about six feet from the floor. Clips were released, and I watched the fluid descend.

At first things went smoothly enough. But about two-thirds down, there was a sharp pain which built up until it became intolerable. I protested, and they stopped. The fluid remained in for twenty minutes, and then was drawn off. I watched warily as the next bottle drained out, waiting for the level to drop to the critical point. I need not have worried. A nurse stopped the flow at the same point as the first. The treatment was to continue for twenty-four hours. Sleep was out of the question: I simply lay and watched.

The word 'dialysis' goes back to a Scotsman from the nineteenth century, Thomas Graham. He stretched some parchment paper over a hoop made of wood. This formed a bowl which he floated in water. Next, he placed a solution of salts and proteins in the bowl. The salts, he noticed, passed through the parchment, but the larger molecules of the proteins did not. He called this process dialysis, and the name has stuck. The experiments done by Graham led rather to the development of the kidney machine than to the type of treatment I was receiving, but the basic principle was the same. Whoever else might grudge Thomas Graham his statue in George Square, Glasgow, I and other kidney patients will not.

Earlier, I said that my trouble was malignant hyper-tension. Actually, the problem had been there long before hyper-tension made its appearance. I had had scarlet fever as a child, and although I enjoyed the time off school which this entailed, the effects of the infection did not end when the symptoms of the scarlet fever left me. A complication arose which affected my kidneys. All through the years from ten to thirty, my kidneys were being gradually destroyed. Since one can carry on quite happily on a quarter of a single kidney, I was totally unconscious of any change. Acne and the growing stubble on my chin, together with the usual neuroses that teenagers pass through, might concern me. The shrinking of my kidneys, their taking on a kind of acne of their own, so that they became pebbly in appearance as the skin shrank down from the dying tissue; the steady approach of end-stage failure; of all this I knew nothing. Now the inevitable hour had come. These burbling bottles and the tube protruding from my body were my one link with life. Who worried about acne now?

The activity of the staff around me stood in complete contrast to my inner feelings. I was the patient. I was suffering the pain. What to the staff was one more routine job, the dismantling of the apparatus, was to me a glorious hour of liberation. The moment came, and nothing happened at first. Then a nurse came in and told me quietly that the urea level was coming down. The treatment was working, and they were going to carry on for another twelve hours. It happened just like that, but there was something shouting within me that I could bear it no longer. Already the first bottle of the new batch was hanging up, and the fluid pouring in.

At times like these, I suppose we should be thankful that decisions are taken out of our hands. My grandmother used to tell of a woman in Lochluichart who was bitten by an adder. She realized that if the poison spread through her system she had little chance of survival. Immediately she cut out the affected area with a knife. Her heroism, the triumph of will over feeling, used to haunt me. But there was nothing so short and sharp in what I was now involved with. Hour after hour through the second night, the pain and discomfort continued. I vaguely remember the dismantling of the apparatus at the end of it: then, I lost consciousness.

When I surfaced, two figures were talking at the foot of my bed.

'How did he come in?' the senior doctor was asking.

'He came in from the Deaconess,' the younger doctor replied. Eventually they left. I was in a semi-conscious state, but that state contrasted with the real world, not as the dimness of the dawn contrasts with the clear light of noonday, but as the ghostly shapes of some dark underworld mimic reality.

I can remember a flurry of questions invading my mind. Who was I? Where was I going? What was my name? Time and space were completely out of joint. I called for the doctor and confronted him with the first question, 'Who am I?' He told me. Then the dialysis experience came back. 'Promise it will never happen again,' I demanded. He promised.

I lapsed back on to my pillow, but my fears and hallucinations did not leave me. In one of these, two spindly giants fought out a duel. Some unidentified calamity was due to occur if one of them won. I believed that a white shape (which I later identified as the globe covering the light) contained a pair of hands. If a certain machine did not arrive in time, the hands would freeze. During this time, I would not smile or speak or take medicine. All this was due, so I have been told since, to the build-up of uric acid in the blood. Usually such a build-up has an unsettling effect on the brain.

It was not long before the big, square bottles were brought in again, and loaded against the side of the wall. Another dialysis was due. I was still in my underworld, still out of contact with reality. One part of my mind told me that I had to get up and replace each bottle with my own hands. Another part was telling me not to be so stupid. No matter how often the nurse came in and changed the bottle, a kind of desperation would build up as each bottle neared its end. I had to change it. Right on time the nurse came in and relieved my anxiety, only for the same concern to build up all over again. (The nurse was a black girl. She sang short snatches of song and then she would stop and turn towards me with a kind of apprehension on her face. Then she would resume her song.)

There were times of lucidity. I woke one day to see my mother and a friend in the corridor. I engaged in conversation before lapsing into unconsciousness again. Another time a minister, the Rev. D. M. MacLeod, due to sail for New Zealand, visited. I recognized him, and was able to talk for a time.

Then I began to respond to kindness once again. I spilt something one time, and confessed to the nurse.

'Don't worry,' she said, 'that's what we are here for.' Another time, blood was being drawn off, and the soft Irish voice of the nurse said, 'I hope it does not hurt.' These were minute things, but to a person who felt within himself that the world had turned bitter and sour, hard and unfeeling, unreasoning and unreasonable, they felt like drops of dew on hard, chapped ground. After weeks of fasting, there came my first meal. It was tea and toast.

'You will not like it much,' said the nurse apologetically. 'The bread is salt free.' At the sight of food, I had the feeling a child must have when faced with some forbidden delicacy.

Dare I touch it? Would I not pay the penalty directly, in vomiting it back up? I ate it, and all was well. (After savouring nothing more exciting than saliva for weeks on end, my taste buds made up for the lack of salt by bringing flavours out of ordinary flour which the baker did not know existed.)

Soon dialysis became a matter of routine, a fact of life, without which I could not exist. There was a certain pride, too, in taking the whole thing quite casually. If I were reading a book when the bottles came in, I tried to seem even more engrossed, and when I had to lay the book aside for the operation to begin, I affected an air of nonchalance. Besides, as far as the doctor was concerned, it was evident that the boring of a hole through the wall of another person's abdomen could hardly have been a pleasant procedure for himself. Hence, there was no sense in making a fuss. The worst part was over in about ten minutes.

There were good dialyses and bad dialyses. They all lasted twenty-four hours. Even under the best I never slept, but could read and, if things went smoothly, could almost forget what was going on. Even at the worst, the first bottle went on quite easily. It was the last few that made the endurance test, before the bottle was slipped out and I was a free agent again; free to enjoy the simple things like turning on my side, or sinking into the oblivion of sleep.

Gradually I was gathering strength. I was able to sit up and look out of the window. This was an important step for me. I could look down to the end of the block and catch a glimpse of the Meadows, where the foliage was still on the trees. I do not suppose we realize how dependent we are on nature until we are taken away from it. In hospital, I was right away from all the normal points of reference which I had been used to.

Life consisted of tubes and medicines, dialysis bottles and the smell of disinfectant. It was a life that turned one in on one's self. What is more, hospital routine had no connection with the normal reference points by which we measure the advance of time. Cycles of nature had meaning for the outside world. Within the hospital, there was no distinction between summer and winter, seed-time and harvest.

Therefore, to sit by the window and watch the trees meant a great deal more than just the opportunity to get a change of position and a different view. It meant a little window through which I could project myself from a world of man's making into the wide world beyond.

14

Brothers in Unity

All the time I felt I was getting better, and there were little indications along this direction each day which kept up my confidence. It was a big day when I was able to go for a shower. Supported by two nurses, I made my way to the end of the corridor where the shower was situated. It soon became a daily event to which I looked forward. I began to badger the nurses to let me outside. Eventually, I got permission. I walked out over the roof of the Infirmary into the fresh air. I would have stayed out longer, but the nurse who accompanied me insisted I turn back.

Yet, despite what I felt to be progress, it must have been about this time that Dr Robson took my mother out and said that if I had come in earlier, something might have been done for me. Now, the illness was too far advanced. There was little prospect, if any, of my recovery.

I, of course, gauged my prospects by my daily improvement. I could now stand in the shower instead of sitting. True, the dialyses continued as regularly as before, but even they were much easier as a result of a protest I made. One particular dialysis was so trying, and I let it be known that the pain was so acute, that the doctor gave me an injection. A pleasing drowsiness followed. By the time the doctor began to work on me he had become a misty, detached figure. Even the most painful period was quite bearable.

I did not ask where all this might end. Peritoneal dialysis, such as I was receiving, was merely a stop-gap. After a time it has to be discontinued. But it was enough for the present that I was able to establish my own routine in my own little world.

When I had reached the stage of getting into the fresh air, I wanted more. I had a craving to see the trees before they lost their leaves that autumn, and winter set in. I was to have a visit from two cousins who were studying in Edinburgh at the time. I wanted to forget that I was in hospital. I would dress normally and walk some distance with them, speaking of family, studies, world events, anything other than life in hospital. Having stood up to the previous walk so well, why should I not go? After some badgering, I did eventually get permission.

The first part, down Middle Meadow Walk, was easy enough. But then my knees became painful; I became weak, and was glad to sit on a bench. The return was up a slight incline, and it was with relief I reached the porters' lodge. I was then able to take advantage of the downward slope to the ward. I was weary, but proud of my accomplishment.

Shortly after, I had dialysis once again. This is one I will never forget. All the time, I was violently sick. Towards the latter part, abdominal pain came in severe spasms. Nothing seemed to relieve it. I wanted the process finished, but was told it must go on. Just when the end seemed in sight, a nurse came in to announce they would have to continue. This was too much. I wanted to see the doctors, and eventually two of them did come in. I hardly looked at them. They departed without promising one thing or another. They must have seen that I was pretty far gone, though, for the nurse came in shortly after and dismantled the apparatus. It would be continued tomorrow, she said. Anything, I thought, provided I get relief now. That must have been very nearly my lowest point.

Out in the corridor, the nurses were laughing and joking. I was no longer on the same plane as they were. I seemed to be sunk at the bottom of a dark well, looking up and up to a bright ring of light far above my head. I could hear laughter, and believe there was sunlight up there, but down in these depths there was only darkness and stagnation and fore-boding. Every peal of laughter I resented with all my heart. I did not envy them their carefreeness; it was just that laughter and jollity did not belong to my world.

A friend dropped by to see me. He was an able raconteur, but I could not concentrate on what he said. I kept dozing, and he soon left. Later at night I felt better, but my old feelings of finding it unbearable to lie in bed made me get up and sit by the door. Something had indeed gone wrong, as an X-ray showed later in the week. I had had a haemorrhage from the stomach, and had to be transfused immediately with four pints of blood. By the end of the week, I had received eight pints in total.

James, my brother, used to come from Bellshill Hospital where he was still working. He had a penchant for old cars, carried over from his student days. (One of my abiding memories from that earlier time was of his disappearing from our home in Dingwall behind a cloud of dust in an ancient Morris 12 which he had picked up for a song. His destination was the distant hills of Sutherland where he had a job for that summer on the Oykell Estate. To get started, this car had to be pushed by whichever members of the family were around, an assistance which would not have been available had it spluttered out into silence again in the midst of some lonely glen. He had, therefore, to keep the engine in life up hill, down dale till he turned off the key at the front door of the hunting lodge.) By now he had graduated to an ancient Rover with the sturdiness of a tank, and doubtless the same voracious appetite for petrol. He used to come in regularly and sit for a time with me. If I felt disinclined to hold a conversation, there was no embarrassment as there might have been with strangers.

Then came the day of the conference. I cannot remember how exactly it came about, apart from the fact that I was asked at one point if I would be willing to have a transplant. There are two ways, it was explained to me, in which one can get a kidney transplant. The kidney can be taken from a person who has recently died (cadaver transplant) or it can be given by a person who has been tested and found suitable (donor transplant).

All four of my brothers had been asked if they were willing to donate a kidney. All had agreed. The compatibility of each had been tested. The kidney of my brother Cameron, a doctor in Aberdeen, had turned out to be most suitable. I was informed by the house-doctor that Professor Woodruff would come up that afternoon to see me and discuss the whole matter.

The side-room that was usually empty became filled with personnel. Dr Lambie was there, and Mr Clark, a surgeon I was to get to know later. Tall, fair-haired and quiet, he stood by the window. The situation was explained to me and I was asked if I had any questions. I asked what the likelihood of success would be, and the relative success of transplant from donor and from cadaver.

'Transplant from a donor has a higher success rate than cadaver transplant,' Professor Woodruff replied. 'When a kidney comes from a donor, the time during which the kidney is not working is kept to a minimum. In your case, given that the kidney would come from a member of your family, the matching would be as close as possible.' He paused, then went on: 'If a suitable cadaver kidney were to become available, would you be willing to accept that?'

'Well, yes,' I answered. 'That would save putting Cameron through a lot.' Professor Woodruff nodded, and there the interview ended as abruptly as it had begun.

It was during the time when I was in the Renal Isolation Unit that I heard that Cameron had decided to get married in Aberdeen. I was asked if I would take the wedding. Naturally, the prospect delighted me. I fixed on Psalm 133 as my text almost before I had begun to think of it. 'How good and pleasant it is for brethren to dwell together in unity! It is like the precious oil upon the head, running down on the beard, the beard of Aaron, running down on the edge of his garments. It is like the dew of Hermon, descending upon the mountains of Zion; for there the Lord commanded the blessing – life for evermore.'

On the outside, all that can be seen when brothers live together in unity is the harmony this brings. On another dimension, however, there is the Holy Spirit descending on each. In the circumstances, I applied this to marriage. Yet I think it may have suggested itself in the first place because of the relationship we as brothers enjoyed with each other.

Because of the closeness of family structure, and the inevitable clash of interests, brothers are notorious for disagreements. We were no exception, though with Cameron's being of a naturally placid temperament and five years younger, our interests did not clash as much as they might have done. Perhaps some might suggest that the equivalent of Mount Hermon and Aaron in our lives was our parents;

and the equivalent of the dew the distilling of their example. I speak for both when I say it went beyond this.

God be thanked for parents who warned and prayed and instructed. All these, however, pointed beyond to a higher source, as Samuel in the temple came to distinguish the voice of God from that of Eli. We, too, came to recognize that what our parents taught us from the Bible came with the authority of God himself.

In my own case, the introduction of this spiritual dimension came through hearing my mother read a simple account of the death of Christ, and the meaning of that death to us as sinners. For some time before, I had been striving upwards towards a life of goodness, only to find myself time and again frustrated in my goal. Prayer was good, I knew, so I tried prayer. My thoughts remained earthbound. Helping others was good, I knew, so I tried in my own simple way to be helpful to my brothers. In a moment of irritation, my carefully constructed efforts collapsed. Only at the moment of hearing that simple account of the death of Christ did I realize what is so evident in Psalm 133: that the power must come from above. I wept, not with frustration this time, but with joy at the simplicity of God's grace.

With Cameron, his entry to this spiritual world came when he was seventeen years old. He was reading a sermon of M'Cheyne's aloud to our grandmother when the meaning of the gospel opened. Thenceforward, we were brothers in more than natural terms.

I was glad the medical staff gave permission for me to go to Aberdeen. It was December 1968, and bitterly cold. With snow on the ground they could have forbidden me. But they didn't, and before long I was in King's College Chapel delivering my address.

The trouble with weddings is, they are over all too soon. Friends and relatives came from north, south, east and west. All my brothers were present apart from Andrew, the oldest, who was in Malawi.

After my incarceration in hospital, I had looked forward to speaking to friends I had not met in years. Most of the hoped-for encounters, however, merely consisted of a smile and a wave across the dinner table. The meal itself was wonderful. I was, of course, on a restricted diet, but the kitchen staff showed their ingenuity both in the variety and tastiness of the dishes they presented within the prescribed limits. I suffered no after-effects. Soon, I was waiting for a taxi to take me to the station.

As I have been writing this, a feeling of frustration has built inside me. It stems partly from the limitations of language. Language can no more express on a two-dimensional page the full flavour of three-dimensional experience than a painter can express the roundness of the three-dimensional world on canvas. The more heavily charged the experience, the less adequate the language.

In dealing with life and death, one is faced with ultimate questions. 'What is life about? Why should I survive, and others not? What is truth?' If I merely describe my own reactions as I went through this valley of the shadow of death, they are almost entirely out of phase with the actual experience. I reacted to situations just as they arose. I showed, I suppose, what people call spirit. When reasonably well, I tried to use what strength I had to the limit. In one way, that can help. In another, it can put one in grave peril if one is careless.

I was in the grip of a mortal disease. Like Leviathan in the Book of Job, who is said to laugh at the shaking of a spear, this illness could scorn my display of spirit. From the depths of my heart, I am thankful that medical treatment was available. Otherwise, I could not have survived. But even the medical staff, with all their expertise, more than once did not expect me to pull through.

Did I really take in the thousand-and-one 'accidents', like the gastric haemorrhage, which might at any moment hurl me over the edge? I did not. Now, I look back as Bunyan's Christian did when in the light of day he surveyed the valley of the shadow of death which he had crossed in the night-time. Many of the things he had feared were, indeed, only phantoms. On the other hand, there were many real pits, into which he came within an ace of falling. His escape from these was no thanks to himself. Ultimately, I can only see God's gracious purposes as the basis of my survival.

I have mentioned the valley of the shadow of death. Christian's valley was, of course, a 'dark night of the soul'. Mine was basically a physical experience, though it did have side-effects in my spiritual life. If we are naturally self-centred, in sickness we are more so. We envy others their health. We wonder why they should have health, and we be denied it. But still God watched over me.

I continued to do well on dialysis. It was proposed that I move from the Renal Isolation Unit in the Infirmary to a side-room in ward twenty-three, the ward which adjoined the Isolation Unit. I welcomed the change, since it would mean much more freedom. I would be able to go out, and visitors could enter without the ritual of donning sterile clothes. Dialysis followed me, but with so much else going on around, the approach of a dialysis session did not loom so large. I developed an absorbing interest in astronomy, fostered by a book on this subject sent by a friend. It was pleasant, while nurses fussed around, and dialysis bottles gurgled out their contents at one's elbow, to lose one's self in the cold waste-lands of outer space. By contrast with the potential for sudden, unpredictable upset in my immediate vicinity there seemed a majestic, calm certainty in the revolutions of stars and planets.

I was quite edgy at the time, as any of the nurses who attended me could testify. I was restricted in my intake of liquids, protein, salt and potassium. With fluids, especially, I tried to extract full measure from the staff. There were not a few arguments as to what constituted two hundred millilitres.

This is the background to my walking over one day to the library on George IV Bridge to get a book on diet values. The library there was a reference one. I was therefore more than surprised when the elderly lady attendant agreed to let me borrow the book and take it back to the ward for a short time. On a subsequent visit, she confessed that the only reason she had stretched the rules was that my complexion was so ghastly and I so evidently sick that she felt it right to do anything she could to help. It was at this time that I said goodbye once and for all to peritoneal dialysis. Neither I nor anyone else was forewarned. Something happened at the beginning of what set out to be a normal treatment. The bottle had emptied only a small amount of its contents when the pain became impossible. The registrar came in. Another attempt was made, with the same result. It was evident the treatment could not continue. It was explained to me that adhesions had probably formed which divided the abdomen into sections. Thus the dialysing fluid was confined to one small part of the abdomen, which became so distended that treatment could not continue. The apparatus was dismantled, and I was promised a place on a kidney machine in the near future.

15

Of Diet and Dialysis

It is quite amazing how one can adapt to a new set of circumstances. I had at one time stumbled into a small room on the top floor of the Infirmary, and drawn back quickly when I saw people with pallid faces laid out on couches. One arm was stretched out, and from one part of this arm a transparent tube evidently containing their blood emerged. Through many loops and coils it coursed as through some bizarre helter-skelter before it disappeared into a giant treble sandwich. At the other end, it emerged again and returned to the arm.

The vision recalled some brave new world from the pages of science fiction. The machine had become dominant; the person was at its beck and call. A process normally done in the secrecy of the body was flung out into the open for all to see. It was the machine which was self-assured, with the steady thrum of its pump, its cool off-white slabs and its dials. Beside it, the body lay languid, weak, passive and totally dependent. Of course, it was simply an impression. The machine was not dominant. The patient might have been relatively helpless, but he was under the watchful eye of the medical staff. And though it might have sucked vampire-like at the life-blood of the patient, it was a kindly vampire. It returned the blood purified, enabling the patient to go on living.

As far as the personal aspect was concerned – the humiliation of dependence on a machine without whose aid life was impossible – it made all the difference simply to be on the receiving end. When one became conscious that one's life was dependent on the operation of such a machine, it became an ally.

The first few times I saw my lifeblood streak along a tube and disappear, I felt more than a pang of uncertainty. I was quickly reassured. After a few moments the blood returned and, at the end of the operation, I received it back again almost entirely. The advantages of being 'on the machine' were immediately obvious. Dialysis itself was a mere nine hours twice a week. I could leave the hospital immediately after. I had been getting out for a day or so at a time previously but now I could stay out every night. The whole procedure was much less harrowing.

Before my first dialysis by machine, a Scribner shunt was fitted. A teflon tube was inserted into the artery on the wrist, lying parallel with the flow of the blood. Another was put into the neighbouring vein. These two tubes were linked by an external bridge of silicone rubber, allowing the blood to flow from artery to vein. When I was not on dialysis, the loop would lay flat on my wrist.

At the time of dialysis this loop could be separated to allow insertion of the tubes which linked the circulation respec-tively to the arterial and venous ends of the machine. The actual machine which performed the dialysis was, in essence, a large steel tub. As the blood flowed through a coil, impurities in the blood were drawn out by osmotic pressure into the surrounding fluid, and the purified blood returned to the body. The fluid in the tub was changed twice, which meant that there were, in all, three periods of purification in the course of one treatment.

My hospital diet had been severely restrained. I was only allowed two cups of any fluid a day. Protein was cut to a minimum; likewise salt and potassium. The staple diet became one boiled egg in the morning, a little meat at lunch with salt-free bread, and some custard. In the evening, there was a set amount of meat or fish again, with more bread. With each meal there was half a cup of tea, and half a cup again at night.

When on the machine, by contrast, diet was free. Breakfast was deferred until after arrival in hospital. One was at liberty, then, to take a breakfast of entirely forbidden foods – porridge, bacon, toast made from ordinary bread, together with multiple cups of coffee. The first three hours were spent in reading and looking forward to a full three-course lunch.

Just before the final stretch of three hours came the deadline. I had to return to a 'normal' diet again. The final course of dialysis took account of all the forbidden foods and excess fluid which had entered my blood-stream in the preceding six hours. Any food taken during the final three hours might cause harm, since digestion would continue beyond the dialysis session, and I would not be able to cope with the by-products, my own kidney function being practically non-existent.

Going into the dialysis room, I had to manoeuvre my way carefully between a large tank of dialysing fluid and the nearest couch, then on to the scales to be weighed. This was the moment of greatest tension. I waited with bated breath to hear the verdict. Since the kidneys could not cope with excess fluid, this merely built up in one's body, and the amount of excess could be read off directly as the level of increase in weight from the previous dialysis. It was a vivid illustration of the text, 'Be sure your sin will find you out.'

Half a cup of water sipped in the corner of the kitchen in the dead of night, when not even the milkman was awake, registered infallibly. Like all judges, the scales were frequently subject to the charge of injustice, and a re-trial claimed by the accused. Sometimes even a change of judge was demanded, and another pair of scales trundled through. In all fairness to the accusers, it was not unknown for the scales to err. Why the fuss? The excess weight put on since the previous dialysis must now come off. It was dealt with by making the solution in the dialysing tank more concentrated than the concentration of the blood by tipping in bottles of dextrose – a form of sugar – into the tub. This exerted a kind of suction on the blood, drawing off excess, until the correct weight was reached. Taking fluid off was an unpleasant procedure. The washed-out feeling which generally followed dialysis was markedly more pronounced, quite simply because the 'washing out' was, in fact, more thorough.

Certainly, there were times when the volcano erupted. I came home one day from dialysis and said to Mother, 'I am not going to stay in Edinburgh tonight.'

'Oh, Fraser!' she replied. 'You can't decide to go off just like that.'

'Why not?'

'Well, it is a bit sudden. Would it not be better to wait till tomorrow?'

'Why should we wait till tomorrow? I've looked into it and I've made up my mind. We can go to Aberlady tonight, stay in Bed and Breakfast, and go on to North Berwick tomorrow.'

Now that the roaming spirit had come, I determined to make the most of the break. This part of Lothian was strange to me, but from the map I could see that Haddington was near at hand. This brought back memories of John Brown, who went from being a shepherd boy to become one of the most influential church figures of his time. Among the hills he learned Greek so quickly, without any assistance, that he was charged with being in league with the devil. We drove down to his home town and asked where he had lived. No-one knew much about him. We were directed to one minister, but he was away from home. The other minister was at home, and showed that our first impressions had been quite mistaken. Brown's name did indeed live on, and we enjoyed a very interesting conversation on his life. His manse was still standing, though the church in which he preached had been converted into a British Legion Hall. A plaque preserved his memory.

Back in Aberlady, there was something of the feeling of the boy who ran away from home and found, to his disappointment, the grass no greener. The view of the flats leading down to the sea was different from the view over the rooftops of Edinburgh. But my condition had changed not a whit. Perhaps it was this I was running away from.

The next day, we went on to North Berwick. It was my ambition to reach the Bass Rock. (Many Covenanters had been imprisoned there. Thomas Hogg, minister in Kiltearn near Dingwall, was one of them.) We found that sailings had been discontinued for the winter. Special parties, however, did go out with ornithologists. Eventually, enough ornithologists were found to make a boat-load. Mother and I tagged on at the end.

A curious mixture: the bird enthusiasts viewed the rock as a kindly sanctuary for the gannets which wheeled about and plunged into the sea around us; we viewed it as a grim jail from which prisoners in the past had looked out in despair over the sea separating them from the mainland.

I sat on the edge of the boat, enjoying the freshness of the sea-air and the occasional dash of spray that came over the bows. Here was complete release from domination by machines! If, in the Renal Isolation Unit, I had looked out with longing on the freedom of nature outside the windows, I was now a participant. The seabirds were hardly more free than I.

After a time, the cold began to seep through. (This, of course, was a direct result of my anaemia. The ability to keep warm relates to the capacity of the blood to carry oxygen. Because my haemoglobin level was low, my ability to carry oxygen was reduced to around 35 per cent of normal, and my body correspondingly more susceptible to cold.) The recipe retained all its ingredients. The sea still slapped against the boat; the engines thrummed; the air was fresh; the scenery perfect. But now, I was retreating. My body was drawing into itself.

In an average person, numbness in hands and feet on a winter's day is evidence of this reaction. To conserve heat in the vital, life-preserving organs, the outposts have to be sacrificed for the time being. The difference in my case was that I was more thoroughly chilled than an average person would ever become, and recovery was a much slower process. An average person might recover in half an hour: I took half a day. I was to find later that hot baths helped when I felt like this, but on this particular day that remedy was out of reach. I just had to sit in the car, no longer trying to persuade myself I should be happy. I sat like a cold-blooded lizard on a rock, gathering as much warmth as I could from the sun and waiting till my temperature reached the level when I would be able to move once again.

More than anything, it was sudden exertion that made me so tired. At rest I could be quite comfortable. It was the moment that I took on an additional workload, especially if the switch from rest to activity were quite sudden, that I found my limitations. The reserves weren't there.

Even when I did undertake projects that seemed sensible and useful, I found the will to persist largely weakened. I tried typing for a while, and various other occupations, but concentration would lag. What would I learn typing for? I had no important, official letters to write.

It was shortly after going on to night dialysis that I got a real nine-to-four job. It lasted all of two days. I had put my name in for temporary teaching at an earlier period. Out of the blue came a request to help in the middle of a 'flu epidemic. When I arrived at the school on Easter Road in the shadow of the Hibs football ground, the staff seemed to have had no prior notice of my arrival. It seemed I was going to be shown the door, but I hung around, and was eventually allocated to a room. The teacher next door introduced me.

'They're pretty tough,' he whispered. To make sure they were properly subdued, he singled out some he evidently thought were potential trouble makers, and gave a demonstration of how to shout them into cowed submission. I could see on his face as he left the room that he had some misgivings as to my ability to keep them in order. 'A semi-invalid, and a clergyman at that!', his expression seemed to say.

I was required to do some readings from Ancient Greek history. Given the personalities of some of the boys involved, I could hardly have thought of anything less likely to stimulate interest. They would be leaving at the end of that particular year and names like Hippocrates, Galen or Euclid would be unlikely to cross their paths again. Yet throughout the lesson, they sat as quietly as a school of philosophers in Athens. They seemed to listen with interest. Was this genuine? Anyway, the spell lasted to the end of the lesson. Thus period followed period to the final bell. That was Thursday. Friday was no less perfect – right to the last lesson.

Then came the deluge. I had had this particular class before, and all had been sweetness and light. Co-operation had been perfect. In all likelihood, in their case, it had been a matter of sizing me up.

I wanted to give them something easy for the final lesson, and even suggested they choose the lesson themselves. That was the beginning. Solemnly they told me they thought they should do a certain lesson which was no more than a giant crossword drawn on the blackboard. The spaces were filled in by the class as a whole. We began well but, before long, anarchy reigned.

One girl was impossible. I would have her sitting quietly one moment, like a model for her portrait. I would half turn away, and she was ranging round the room on the tops of the desks. Mutiny reigned as far as answering the questions was concerned. To keep face, I had to supply nearly all the answers myself. When I turned my back on them to write the answer on the board, a shower of pencils descended on me through the air like so many arrows. My carefully modulated voice went to the winds. There was one consolation. This was the last period of the day, and would be my final period of teaching. I departed with my estimation of the teaching profession considerably heightened.

It was only in such tiny ways that I was able to launch out into the main tide of life again. Hardly had I done so, however, when I had to retreat. I found that, as an invalid, I was repeatedly forced to turn back in on myself.

Because my haemoglobin level was low, I was at this time being starved of oxygen. The first part of the body to feel this is the brain. Dizziness follows any unusual exertion. While on the kidney machine, a tendency to dizziness is further increased because so much of one's blood is out of service at any particular time. It is circulating through the machine, undergoing treatment. When I lay flat, there was little danger of a black-out. However, there were two intervals when the dialysing fluid was changed, and at these points I was weighed.

Sitting on a weighing machine might not seem the ultimate in energy-sapping activities, but dizziness would begin when I sat on the scales. I would then drift away, as though wafted by some invisible wind. There was no coercion, just a gentle uplifting. Nor was there any need for alarm since, on lying down, the process was reversed, and I drifted back again. The sensation could actually be quite enjoyable. Sometimes, however, the experience was not so pleasant, as the following note testifies:

> *I am writing this on the machine. I have just been weighed, and felt dizzy. After lying down I felt very uncomfortable with that strange feeling that dizziness brings on. It is as though one's personality were breaking up into pieces. There was a sense of facing reality – this is the ultimate end. Death must be like this – like a horror of darkness, as though one were going into some cave with unknown dangers before one, and all the time*

*reaching backwards, clinging to the light. I banged my fist
on the wooden support beside the chair. It was not an act
of defiance. Rather, it was, 'Is this all, after life with all its
varied interests? Is the materialist right when he says the
spiritual has no independent existence, and when the
physical breaks up, it also goes? Is to exercise faith merely
to nurse an illusion so carefully that it becomes part of
one's self?'*

Perhaps one is not expected to write these things. But
then, if so, Jeremiah would never have left on record that he
cursed the day of his birth, and Asaph would never have
disclosed that at a particular time he questioned whether
there were knowledge in heaven of things below, and Job
would never have said, 'Behold, I go forward, but he is not
there.'

16

Those Who Stand and Wait

One thing which made such experiences on the machine easier to tolerate was the fact that the next cubicle might well contain a person going through experiences even more harrowing.

Barbara would be sick almost directly after going on and, as often as not, missed our luxury of a normal meal at lunchtime. It helped when she came to know the nurses better, and brought photographs of her children to show around. Shortly after, she had the excitement of a new house to talk about.

There was always competition as to who would be on the machine first. The process of releasing a person from the kidney machine took half an hour per person, and was performed on each individual according to the time of arrival. All four might arrive within the space of ten minutes, but there was a difference of two hours between the commencement of the release of the first and the time when the last could leave the ward. By that time nerves were becoming frayed, and captivity correspondingly irksome.

There was a slight incline from the ward up to the road, and I could always judge how much the dialysis had taken out of me by how far I could walk without becoming dizzy. One stop at least was inevitable, and I got a little canvas stool I could unfold and use as my staging-post. Later, I found an easier route along corridors, past the shop, and out the side door. I dispensed with my stool, since there was always a convenient window-sill on which to rest. Once settled in the car, I drove home without difficulty. I cherished that little bit of independence I preserved in making my way home by myself. If I really needed help from Mother, it was easy enough to phone.

When I first had got out, a few days at a time while in Ward 23, I had stayed in Dick Place with the Mackay family. After the institutional atmosphere of the hospital, I had welcomed heartily the warmth of a family circle.

I owe much to the Mackays for making a place for me. Mr Mackay – now Lord Mackay – had a busy law practice as a Queen's Counsellor. At tea-time, when he did respond to the call from the dining room, he would often enter the room with a far-off, preoccupied air. If one peeked into the study, the reason would be clear to see. A good variety of the law books which normally lined the walls with the regularity of soldiers on parade would be adopting various undignified postures anywhere from the floor to the corners of the desk. But he could quickly switch off and enter freely into the mood of the company in which he found himself.

Sometimes, dialysis went easily. Sometimes, I was glad to roll into bed as soon as I returned. Whatever the situation, it was good to be able to relax. However, I found myself wakening in the middle of the night. When this happened, I used to get up and read by the fire. The book that stands out in my memory is Krummacher's *The Suffering Saviour*. The stillness of the night in Dick Place, the freedom from distraction, made me more receptive. My own illness also made me more responsive to the theme. Perhaps this may seem to contradict what I have written already as to illness unfitting one for spiritual exercise. Of the raw experience of illness, I found that this was so. Nevertheless, as Wordsworth spoke of poetry as emotion recollected in tranquillity, so I found that recollection of suffering afterward, when one had had time to assimilate the experience, deepened one's appreciation for the suffering of Christ – the recoil from the evil of suffering, and yet the ready acceptance of it in love for his church. I almost looked forward to these nightly interludes, and found it relatively easy to return to sleep again.

The arrangement with the Mackays could not continue indefinitely. Towards the end of 1968 my mother came down to look after me and we tried to find a flat. A few members of the family gathered to discuss what we should do. A couple from Edinburgh called to see us, but when they heard that the family were all together they turned to leave. Mother followed after them. As she explained why we were having this discussion, the husband turned to his wife.

'Could we help?' he asked.

'I think we could,' she replied. The couple were James and Kathleen Taylor. They had converted the top floor of their house in Garscube Terrace into a flat, expecting that James' mother would come down from Caithness to stay in it. Mrs Taylor had in fact come down from Halkirk to Edinburgh, but her tenancy of this flat had only lasted three months. One cannot overnight forget the seventy years one has lived in a cottage on the edge of a Caithness village, nor the friends one has made, nor the memories that linger in the mind, nor the smell of a spring morning when the larks take to the sky, nor the lash of rain in winter when the fire is roaring in the grate. Only when one makes the move does one realize how one's personality has been honed over the years to fit this place and this alone.

Mrs Taylor's departure created our opportunity and the arrangement, from our side, was quite ideal. It was the utmost kindness, not to say faith, which opened the door for us into that house in Garscube Terrace. I was in the middle of a course of treatment of which there was no certain end. It would have been very much easier to pass by on the other side. If involvement in their own interests might have been pleaded as reason to take no action, James Taylor's position as headmaster of Tynecastle School, and Kathleen's as mother of a family of four would have been enough. Instead, we were welcomed freely and without fuss.

From the back of the flat, practically all Edinburgh landmarks were in view – the Castle, St Giles' Cathedral, Donaldson's School, etc. St George's School was just outside the window, across a disused railway line. But the view from the front of the flat in Garscube Terrace was particularly attractive. After a day on the machine, I could sit back and look out at Corstorphine Hill, with that mysterious quarry – rendered mysterious by distance itself – up in the foothills of the Pentlands. In the middle distance, trains snaked their way along the line to the West. At the same time I would resent that I could not be part of this scenic world.

I do recollect how thoroughly enjoyable the first train journey was when I could look out at vistas that reached the horizon, and feel something of the buzz of life around me. But I was no real participant in that activity. For the businessman, the tradesman and the schoolchild, the journey was meaningful because it had a meaningful end. I was the odd man out. The run had to be an end in itself.

[106]

I can remember pausing one time before entering the dialysis area, and looking through the glass partition at all the activity within. A kind of wall built up in my mind. Here I was alone in the corridor. I had a moment of reflection, thinking 'Is it all worth it? You are a free agent now, but the moment you enter, you will find yourself on a human conveyor belt. You will be weighed, your pressure taken, laid on a bed, connected to a machine. What kind of night will you have? You may come off feeling thoroughly ill. Is it worth it? Why go in at all?'

John Milton, the poet, knew the continual struggle with the constant disability of his blindness. I'm sure it was more than once he had to still himself in 'patience to prevent his murmur'. Many times he would have returned to his reasoning:

> God doth not need
> Either man's work or his own gifts. Who best
> Bear his mild yoke, they serve him best. His state
> Is kingly; thousands at his bidding speed,
> And post o'er land and ocean without rest;
> They also serve who only stand and wait.

I could not reach Milton's poetic vision. But then, I am sure he himself must as often have struggled through the dark in faith as he was borne aloft on triumphant wings.

My life was not totally dominated by the dialysis unit, though. I wanted to preach again, and found that my services could be employed in Dumbarton. I stayed with various members of the F. P. congregation there. I owe them thanks for making it possible for me to have this form of occupational therapy. It cannot have been easy for them. I remember excusing myself from the tea table one evening. I meant to lie down in the bedroom, but only got as far as the hall, where I collapsed. By the next morning, I was none the worse.

Then there was the prospect of my brother Andrew returning from Malawi on furlough. I had just missed him when I returned from Canada. Now, almost three years later, he was due to come back again. He sent word that he wanted us to be on the lookout for a house for him. My mother and I looked up the columns of the Evening News, and gradually became reasonably adept at eliminating the obviously undesirable. But finding a house was more difficult than we had suspected. I am not sure whether it was an advantage that there were two of us searching. If I would declare a place highly desirable because of the view from the front room, Mother would almost certainly find the kitchen dingy, and the cooker old-fashioned. The days ran on, and suddenly Andrew and Beth were on the doorstep, and still no house. It was probably just as well. They did their own house-hunting from that day forth, and got what suited themselves.

It was about this time, while I was on dialysis, that the tall fair-haired surgeon, Mr Clark, who had stood at the window while the possibility of a transplant was being discussed, came round the beds. In his early thirties, he was about my own age. To him I owed two elongated scars which ran down each of my wrists, the result of the insertion of my two shunts. He was reserved, but the success of his work spoke for him. I watched him move from bed to bed, secretly wishing I might have a visit myself. A visit from such a senior medical figure could indicate a new development of some kind; one never knew what. He did stop. Arms folded in a characteristic stance, he said:

As they have probably told you, they'll be doing your transplant when the unit opens again. At present it is closed for alterations, and it's taking longer to complete than we anticipated.

The expression on his face hardly indicated a flicker of emotion. I hadn't heard a word of this news before, but I can remember the sense of quiet joy that entered. The surroundings of the dialysis unit were hardly the place for exuberance, and the quiet, matter-of-fact way the news was conveyed would hardly in itself stir one to a pitch of excitement; but my elation, lacking effervescence, was there all the same.

So the decision had been taken. This long tunnel was at last to have an ending. I knew that Cameron, down on a visit earlier, had seen the surgical authorities in the Western General and discussed the matter with them. He had renewed his request that his kidney be used for my transplant. I had heard no more, and had no reason to think that his earlier offer would be acted on. I could hardly wait till the morning to tell Mother the good news.

Eager anticipation was increased by bits of news which came my way about others who had benefited from a transplant. One patient, Charlie, had been with me in the Renal Isolation Unit. He had come in critically ill. I had seen him lie on his dialysis couch, thin and emaciated, with his head slung to the side on his pillow. He was an in-patient at this point. He had to be. His life consisted of going a few steps to be dialysed, and then returning to bed again. Even this he could not do without assistance. He showed no flicker of interest in anything. He only wished to be left to sleep, and the nurses had difficulty in cajoling him into rising at all. He disappeared from the dialysis unit, and we discovered that he had gone for a transplant.

One night Dr Bone came in, highly pleased. He seemed to have good news he wanted to convey to someone. The nursing staff at the desk got the benefit, and by a little eavesdropping I could make out the gist of his message. He had just seen Charlie sitting up in bed devouring a huge meal. He had altered out of all recognition.

I found myself counting the weeks like a child who has just received the good news that he is to be let home from school. There was to be one further hitch, however, on the count-down to the transplant. One Sunday, when I happened to be at home, there came a phone call. Dr Bone was speaking.

> Fraser, there is a kidney available, and it is possible that it might be suitable for you. Come up to the Infirmary, and we will take off some blood to test whether it matches.

My brother Andrew was staying in Edinburgh at this time. We phoned over, and he came immediately to drive me up. We waited outside Ward 21. There was a bustle of activity for, in addition to the usual work of the ward, all on the transplant list who might be able to use the kidney were being contacted. Blood was taken, and I returned home. I would hear later whether I or some other person had been chosen. At that point I hoped it would be me, since this would save Cameron the trauma of an operation to extract his kidney, and would mean that the build-up to my transplant, which would put stress on everyone, would be bypassed. In less than twenty-four hours the operation would be over and done with.

In the evening, I waited across the fire from my Aunt Helen. Neither of us spoke much. We were absorbed in our own thoughts. I had had no food since, if the operation were to be done, it would be done that night, and nothing must be eaten before it. When it came, the phone call would mean either a sudden burst of activity, or else nothing more than a meal, and then bed. Shortly, the tension was broken. A brief word on the phone informed me that the kidney had been given to a man from Dundee. Unlike the others who would have been disappointed at not getting that particular kidney, however, I had the certain prospect of having one in the near future.

I was reasonably well for a dialysis patient, but the prospect of regaining my freedom, and a much higher standard of health, on the other side of a five- or six-week stay in hospital, was so alluring that I could overlook the un-pleasantness of confinement.

One day, when Andrew and I were standing outside the house which he had bought in Comiston Springs Avenue, Andrew remarked that, when I was better, after the operation, I could stay there with Mother. The offer was extremely kind. Yet, it was not the offer which struck me. It was that part, 'When you are better.' It had seemed so unattainable, and now it was almost within my grasp. I looked down the road from the front door of the house, and needed no biblical expositor to explain how such contrary emotions as 'fear and great joy' may coexist, as in Matthew 28:8. I had them within myself.

By this time I was receiving dialysis in the Transplant Unit of the Western General Hospital, where my operation was due to take place. One wall of the room I occupied there consisted almost entirely of plate glass. In order to keep the room scrupulously sterile, communication between the patient and the outside world was by means of an intercom which was built into the plate glass.

My wait in the Transplant Unit was extended since, at the last minute, the head of the Unit had himself to go through an operation. This was Professor Woodruff, a pioneer in the study of organ rejection. The registrar brought the news:

> Mr Nolan will do the main operation on you now, and we are trying to find a senior surgeon who will operate on Cameron. If we cannot find one, we will have to defer the date.

At one point, I thought I might have to leave the Unit and wait for a further period. I felt most unwilling to do this. I had tallied up the number of dialysis treatments I had yet to undergo, and felt I had the patience to bear just that number and no more. Doubtless, I could have wound down my keyed-up expectancy and become resigned to a deferment; but some inner mechanism had started a countdown, and any suspension would have meant complete readjustment.

Eventually, the last dialysis was over. It was entirely uneventful. I only remember waking up after it was finished and seeing the technicians dismantling the apparatus on the other side of the glass screen which divided me from the outside world. They took down the polythene tubing, and trundled away the apparatus in the most matter-of-fact way; all in a day's work. It was all routine for them, but for me it was a landmark: it symbolized the dismantling of a way of life which I had followed, or which had followed me, over the past year.

I could not enumerate the benefits I owed to it. I owed my life to it. The last few months had brought pain and sickness, but the final dialysis had been trouble-free.

Yet, I had been chained, and I felt rather like a colonial country on the day of its independence. No matter what benefits the mother country has conferred, no matter how the colony has been nourished, cherished and even pampered, the only thought that day is of independence. That was the one word which rang most in my mind as I saw the steel tub disappear round the corner, and heard the rumble of its wheels die away in the distance. Then my reverie was broken as the nurses came in to turn my bed round, back to the wall again.

Cameron, who was to give his kidney, had come down to Edinburgh. It was all the more to Cameron's credit that his gift was not merely an emotional response to the need of a brother. As a doctor, he was giving his kidney in the full knowledge of what this would mean to him. He had attended lectures on transplant, and, rather than drawing back, was the more willing to be a donor.

One visiting hour before he came into hospital, Mother, Andrew, and Cameron himself were standing outside the glass. Alongside was an easel and blackboard on which the diagram of a kidney was sketched. It had probably been used in teaching students.

Conversation was rather slack, and I asked Cameron to give us a tutorial on the anatomy and physiology of the kidney. He soon had us lost among the convoluted tubules and glomerular corpuscles, but it was interesting to follow as we could and served to heighten, for me, the value of the gift I was to receive.

17

The Gift

Day after day, the countdown continued. Cameron was admitted to his own room next door to mine. I was sorry I had never mastered Morse Code, or we could have communicated by means of banging on the wall.

The day finally came when I was wheeled out into the central corridor and across to the anaesthetics room. I cannot pretend I was without trepidation, but the anaesthetist had come round beforehand, so I knew him when his face swam into view. There was the usual warning of the little prick, and I was submerged before I knew it.

I woke up back in the room. Underneath a slanting scar on the right side of my abdomen was a kidney which had operated for 26 years inside the body of my brother. In all probability, it had never had to deal with a concentration of urea in the blood above 40 mg, and then only in conjunction with a fellow kidney on the other side. Now, without any assistance, it was purifying blood with a concentration of over 200 mg. My two diseased and shrivelled kidneys which had, in effect, died themselves had been bypassed. I now had a kidney five years younger than myself which, amazingly, was a part of me and did the work of purification on my behalf.

The gift of Cameron's kidney, in November 1969, came to me with a sense of bounding joy. I had a dream about this time. I was back in Kames, where I was born, on a patch of cement at the back door which we called 'The Concrete'. Some sinister visitors arrived, and I went into the house. The details are blurred, but I do remember that the action thereafter centred around a certain piece of meat which had become soiled, and therefore useless.

Suddenly someone took the meat to the sink, which was just inside the back door, and scrubbed it clean. At this, a sense of elation seized me. The dark foreboding was gone. I ran out on to the concrete and began dancing. The dream was vivid, but it took a little reflection when I awoke to establish the connection. The cleansing of the meat represented the new kidney, with its power to cleanse my body. The leaping for joy was, of course, metaphorical. I was firmly anchored to my bed by five tubes which emerged from different parts of the site of the operation, and ran into bottles which jangled on the side of my bed each time I moved.

Ward Sister Weatherstone suggested getting me up on the second day. I did not like to question her judgment, but when she left I could only look despairingly at my various appendages draped around the bed and wonder how they could come along, too. Would I need five train-bearers to accompany me on this walk? I dozed off and had a most dreadful nightmare in which I tumbled helplessly down a series of stairs. As with the other dream, I did not immediately grasp the meaning, but when I told it to Sister Weatherstone on her return shortly after, she realized my sub-conscious fear. 'We'll leave you till tomorrow,' she said. The next day I had my walk, and with it came a new sense of confidence.

It was only after the operation was over that I saw Mr Nolan, the surgeon who had performed it. He appeared outside the glass, with others of the medical staff. I could identify him because the others stepped back to let him come forward and speak. He pressed the button of the intercom, and the voice came through, precise and correct.

'How are you?' How strange it seemed! I had never before seen him, and knew nothing of him. Yet in a certain way he knew me more intimately than I did myself. For five hours he had traced the paths of blood vessels I had never seen, and would never see. He had taken Cameron's kidney and stitched its blood vessels to my own. I felt a surge of gratitude I could not express. Even if I tried to smile, my facial muscles would not obey me. I was still in shock from the operation.

Time has dimmed the memory of these first few days. There was the constant taking of blood pressure, and the immediate injection if it had risen too high. One after another the drains came out, till only one remained. It was due for extraction ten days from the operation.

Towards the end of these ten days, in one of these un-accountable depressions, my spirit did fail. I suppose it is typical that, just at the time when things are going to turn for the better, one's nerve can falter. I had come through the worst, but now there seemed to be a reaction. A wall seemed to be building up, and suspicion about the success of the operation began to assail me.

The straw that broke the camel's back came when one of the staff mentioned casually that since my pressure was not coming down, they would probably have to remove my own two kidneys. (Apparently they were secreting an enzyme that was causing my continuing high blood pressure.) For some hours I sank into a Slough of Despond. Yet that evening, as I padded around my enclosure, I was conscious that something was better. Whether my mental improvement corresponded to some physical change within, I could not say. I only knew that I had turned some corner, and the path ahead seemed clear. The isolation did not help my spirits. It meant that I was cut off from many who, I knew, were remembering me in prayer. I am sure that in ways unknown to me, and indeed unknown to them, their prayers helped to relieve my spirits.

One visit I looked forward to was that of the physiotherapist. If any physiotherapist wished to find her calling, I was an ideal specimen. My muscles sagged from their tendons like bow-strings that had lost all their elasticity. I was three stones below my usual weight. Daily, the physiotherapist came round and put me through a strict regimen – walking, heaving weights, bending, standing up. I inwardly rebelled at first. The languid pose of the invalid had been so natural to me for so long. I thought it only just that I should not tax my meagre resources.

Now I was expected to toil through exercises four times a day. I was spending one and a half hours on exercise alone. But the single thing that was needed to give me incentive had happened. I was getting stronger. My muscles flexed with ease as I swung bags of lead-shot from my legs, or lifted them with my arms. I developed poise in walking. The ground did not seem ready to crumble under my feet, as I had felt it seem to do so often before.

Once I felt reasonably well, visitors were always welcome, though the frustration of the glass wall was always there. My relatives kept up a faithful attendance. Then, one day, a group of distinguished guests arrived from England. One was the President of the Royal College of Surgeons. They came round the corner, all of them with their individual consultant stance developed over the years. Some, with shoulders hunched, looked over half-moon glasses. Others were more relaxed, and seemed to aim rather at putting the patient at ease. There they were, a concentration of medical talent, momentarily directing their attention at me. It was the building they had come to visit, though. Apparently the Renal Isolation Unit in the Western General was one of the few which had been built specifically for transplant surgery. Behind the stance which was adopted as a matter of course, the minds of these men of medicine would have gone on holiday. Cameron left after ten days.

Sometime thereafter, a little patient who had previously received a transplant came in. She was a young girl, with the typically puffy face of someone on large doses of steroids. She had had her transplant two years before, and had been given such a concentration of steroids at the time that her growth was stunted. She was up and about every day, and I sometimes waved to her as she passed the glass on a walk, hand in hand with her father. She was quiet and retiring.

One day Sister Weatherstone took her out for the day, and as she passed my room on the way back, she paused for a talk. She was evidently thrilled by her day off. But in the middle of speaking, overcome by shyness, she broke off to run back to Sister Weatherstone. Once we met in the corridor, where she squatted over a jigsaw. I sat for a moment and helped her while we chatted patient to patient about inconsequential things, glad at least to make the human contact. It was to the nurses she spoke more than to me, and to them she was quite free about her worries for her family, especially for her father, since her mother had already died.

It is when one meets a girl like this that one realizes how wrong it is to speak in any cold, measured terms of 'quality of life'. With all our emphasis on technology and IQ tests, we want the value of everything to be spelt out in easily accessible terms. In terms of IQ, Margaret would have rated very low. In relation to a job, or even recreation, her prospects would have been correspondingly poor. Yet, as she walked silently hand in hand down the corridor with her father, or told in broken sentences, with a kind of suppressed excitement, of her day out with Sister Weatherstone, Margaret's personality clearly occupied a niche none other could fill. When I returned on one of my first out-patient visits to the Unit, I heard the niche had become empty. Margaret had died.

It was mainly to books, supplied by friends and relatives, I had to look for interest in those days of confinement. They were baked – yes, baked – in an oven over an appropriate length of time to ensure there would be no contamination from the Great Untamed Beyond.

One book that made a deep impression on me was the life of James Renwick, the last of the Covenanters to be martyred. On a visit to Edinburgh in 1688, he was caught after a chase in the lanes and back-streets of the city. Only twenty-six years old, he died on the gibbet in the Grass-market. Many, even some who sympathized with the general principles for which he fought, dubbed him an idealist, an enthusiast, a fanatic. Yet, as I read his letters, I saw the dedication that inspired him. He was a young man with all the natural enthusiasm of youth. Yet that enthusiasm poured out in one direction, towards the service of Christ and his 'suffering remnant'. There was one passage in particular that remained with me. He exhorted his correspondent to give all for Christ – riches, lands, houses, etc. The climax was, 'The travail of our souls, let it be his.'

Is it any wonder that the contrast between my position and his raised questions in my mind? He was in perfect health, and willingly gave his life at about the same age as I was recovering my own. But recovering for what? What was to be my quality of life? Was it to be measured in terms of a perfect blood count, a normal blood pressure, or should there be more? There was in his case. His dedication carried him beyond thought of personal safety to the point where death was willingly accepted rather than renunciation of principle. Here was quality of life expressed in higher rather than physical terms.

As I looked out through the big flat plate of glass to the outside world where I would shortly go, I was forced to wonder what use I was to make of the gift of restored health. What value would my own life have? This was a question which allowed of no pat answer. But whatever the gap between Renwick's time and mine, however great the differences in detail between his life and mine, of one thing I felt assured: following Christ is synonymous with taking up the cross.

When I had left the Unit, and was staying in my brother's house in Comiston Springs Avenue, I took a walk over the Braid Hills. Lurking in the back of my mind was the old feeling: 'It can't last. Something is going to snap.' Nothing snapped. I climbed dykes, went up hill and down dale, and felt as fit at the end of the exercise as at the beginning. My watch alone pointed to the passage of time and the necessity to return to the house. No-one was at home when I walked through the door. I went over to the record-player, and put on a record of hymns. The first was 'Rock of Ages'.

It was not the words that caught me. The music itself seemed to arch over me like a canopy, and under this canopy my innermost feelings felt safe to come out and express themselves. They did so in a copious outpouring of tears.

On the hills I had sensed the indescribable value of life, the privilege of having health restored. As illness is an indefinable something that gnaws at the vitality of one's spirit, so health seemed to be a voice, an unspoken presence walking with me, lightly taking my hand, saying, 'I have returned. You are whole now, you are whole. You have no need to fear.' Why, then, the tears? That gift I saw to be so immense, so indescribable, that I knew I would never be able to use it to its fullest potential.

While in the Unit, I had watched a clip on television about a book shortly to be published, called *Selected to Live*. It spoke of a Jewess hunted by the Nazis in Holland. Wonder of wonders, she had become a Christian. As she looked back over experiences which she had survived when others had not, she could only say, 'There but for the grace of God go I.' Like the psalmist in the 124th Psalm, she united relief, 'Our soul has escaped as a bird from the snare of the fowlers', with praise, 'Blessed be the Lord, who has not given us as prey to their teeth.'

There is no need to underline the parallels to my own case. That I had received treatment at all was a wonder. At that time only 10 per cent of those with renal failure were given the treatment I received. Peritoneal dialysis worked for me, and provided relief when no other was available. And then I had been given a place on a kidney machine. Of the four who had shared dialysis with me, only I survived. Mr Corbett died of Hepatitis B. (This illness accounted for more than patients. Even the fair haired surgeon, Mr Clark, was struck down. The Greek house-doctor who attended to me in the Unit also became a victim.)

I had ascites (fluid in the abdomen) as Barbara, a fellow patient, had; but I did not die as she did. I had blood transfusions, but none of the blood specimens was infected.

Like Ruth Dobscheiner, the Jewish lady, I could only look back and say, 'Praise be to God.'

18

Looking Back

The transplant operation took place in November 1969. Dating my recovery from 1970, I now look back in 1992 on those days of illness, through one year spent in Aberdeen, nine in Broadford, Skye, and twelve in Kinlochbervie. I was healed in body, but there was a whole variety of ways in which I was maimed, dragging the experience of the past years with me into the present.

There was a social worker who interviewed me once or twice. I cannot admit to receiving much help. It seemed almost as though she, herself, were uncertain how to proceed. She had a bright smile, and yet that smile itself was a barrier. It indicated, 'I wish to please. I wish to be of service.' Perhaps if I had begun to tell something of my inner thoughts, she would have become more serious and descended with me into some of the dark caverns below the surface. But the smile kept putting me off. If I were to go back in there, I wanted someone to hold my hand, and she was not the one to do it. Hence we looked at each other and nodded and we both smiled and parted the best of friends and the dark, dark places remained as secret as ever.

I can well understand the rationale behind using dogs to help people in stress. What they need, from a psychological point of view, is to express the stress they feel in a non-threatening environment. A dog does not speak. He is just there. He is there to be loved. He loves whatever mood one is in. The quiet devotion of his eyes says enough. Verbalization is so dangerous. One word spoken in a threatening, condemnatory, condescending, supercilious or inquisitorial way is like a clap of thunder to a vulnerable person.

Someone spoke to me about death as a triumphant experience. It was like that for the martyr Stephen as he stood looking upwards, full of the Holy Spirit, saying 'Look! I see the heavens opened and the Son of Man standing at the right hand of God!' But I, too, had brushed with death and, for myself, I had found it anything but a triumphant experience. There was a direct connection between this and my writing a poem called *The Martyr*. In this poem, I sought to express the conflicts felt by a man who was called to lay down his life. I spoke of his final triumph, but it was when I spoke of conflict that I truly identified – and wept – with him.

> *Bass,*
> *Deep bass,*
> *Ascending,*
> *Securing every step in his advance,*
> *Voice resonating.*
>
> *Whence comes this great Goliath?*
> *He strains to see the face,*
> *But it is featureless,*
> *No ears to hear and reason with,*
> *No eyes to see.*
> *A stone the only remedy;*
> *He slings,*
> *'Have thine own way, O Lord,*

Have thine own way.'
In desperation, now,
'Have thine own way.'

David should slay Goliath;
This one merely divides,
Quadruples, multiplies
Into a chorus of a thousand voices,
A thousand longings, aspirations unfulfilled
Mouthing protest.

In this, I was doubtless reflecting my experience as recorded in the diary entry, written while on the kidney machine. Then, and on many other days during my illness, any resolving of my conflicts was a matter of faith rather than of experience.

I had to readjust to being a minister again. This was not just a matter of praying and preaching. In many ways, the experience of sickness made these easier. I preached around the time of my convalescence on Psalm 63, 'Because your love is better than life, my lips will praise you.'

It may seem surprising, when I have been so negative in describing my spiritual state while physically unwell, that my illness helped me to tackle such an exalted subject. The negative experiences came because the implications of following Christ are pressed home in illness. In all these, there was the insistent question, 'Now do you believe?' In all, there was a conflict. 'Without were fightings, within were fears.' But at the deepest level, when the dust had cleared away, I could say, 'Lord, you know all things; you know that I love you.' I almost tremble to say this. To have stood up and said it at the time would have invited a backlash. My conscience might have charged me with hypocrisy. It was easier to preach it as the experience of the Psalmist, and to add my own 'Amen' to his. At one stage during my illness, the niece of a friend visited Edinburgh. She had just lost her young husband in an accident. I preached on 'Jesus wept', and if the sermon grew in the highest sense from a consciousness of the compassion of Christ, and from a sense of personal sympathy with her, it grew also from my own experience of suffering.

On another occasion during my illness, I preached on Pilate's words to the Jews about Christ, 'Behold the man.' The pathetic figure of Christ, wounded, displaced, disowned, was the subject of my sermon. An awareness of my own problems added to my identification with the subject.

After recovering from the transplant I should have gone off on a break, but did not. I had much readjustment to do, and it would have been better done right away from hospitals. Instead, I stayed on in Edinburgh for the first few months, and then went up to Aberdeen to take the services for the infant F. P. congregation there. I really should have given myself space to re-think the whole direction of my ministry. I had been living under considerable pressure in Winnipeg. I had gradually come to some conclusions as to how I should conduct my ministry, and was attempting to reduce these to practice. In many ways, I could see a new direction was needed if the congregation were to survive. (They have since folded.) There needed to be more identification with people where they were rather than where, ideally, we thought they should be. I had, indeed, become somewhat disenchanted with the operations of the home church in this respect. With my illness, all this went underground. If any person was thankful for the ties that bind Christians together, that person was me. I knew the volume of prayer that was offered up for me. While I was undergoing treatment, there was no need for me to question where our Church was going. Only when, with the return of health, I was called to rejoin the team of ministry in the Church, did the old questions resurrect themselves.

In May following my operation, I was now fit enough to attend the annual Synod. A Resolution was put forward condemning racial disharmony as sin, and saying the gospel was the only answer. All was perfectly correct and scriptural, and yet within me it was as though a rocket exploded. I had met some church people in Canada who would say correct things, and even pray earnestly in the most correct manner, but when it came to direct involvement, when it came to reducing principles to practice, there was a speedy retreat behind a 'form of sound words'. Perhaps my reaction was an over-reaction, but I could not help saying to myself, 'What do we know of racial tensions, living as we do in the Scottish Highlands? Until we answer questions of a practical nature, what is the value of resolutions so general that all, without question, would agree to them? How can we begin to touch the needs of modern society until we let these tensions first touch us?'

Shortly after this I walked out with a friend along a path at Cramond. The trees to me had the swirling branches of a van Gogh picture, restlessly turning and twisting. My friend could not identify with my mood. Only when we returned to the car, and we both bowed our heads in prayer, did I find some peace. After a crisis in his ministry, the prophet Elijah went off into the wilderness, to Horeb. There, his inner tensions were brought out and dealt with, and the way forward was mapped out. I should have found my own personal Horeb. I didn't, and that meant periods of depression after lunchtime when, in Aberdeen, I would thrash myself through crowds of shoppers in the superstores, attempting to shake off the dark moods that haunted me. It meant waking in the night with nameless fears. It meant a hyper-sensitivity to suffering.

I remember one particular experience of this kind. I was waiting at a bus-stop when a disabled man joined the queue. A sense of compassion welled up within me toward this man. I felt I had to express some solidarity with him. I surprised myself by going towards him and giving him some money. He received it graciously, and no-one else in the bus queue seemed to notice.

Perhaps, as much as anything, there was the difficulty of not dealing with life as a series of emergencies any more. That had been the story of my illness. One emergency had followed another, emergencies that needed rapid solutions. Either emergencies had just been overcome, or further emergencies were around the corner. As months passed, this evolved into a way of life. Anything more different from my way of life in Canada could not be imagined. There, I have described my work rather like that of the cart-horse who patiently pulls away. Now that I was well, I had to wind back down to that kind of style, and it was not easy.

I was inclined to lunge at problems, rather than tackle them piece by piece, according to a regular plan. That might have been due in part to my personality. In athletics, I used to be a sprinter rather than a long-distance runner. No wonder it was difficult for me to develop the image of the cart-horse. After my illness my whirls of activity were more intense; and my whorls of depression, when things didn't work out, deeper. I didn't take my holiday.

And yet, after all, it's 1992 and here I am. 'Having therefore obtained help of God, I continue to this day.'

Part Three

THE STORY CONTINUED

19

Fraser's Later Years

Although Part Three continues the story, this chapter begins by looking again, from a different perspective, at some aspects of the period already covered. In Part One we reached the stage where Mother had begun to sell Christian books in Dingwall. At first she did this from her small upstairs flat, but as time passed she moved her tiny business into a room off the High Street. She was just beginning to get this fledgling project established when she heard from Canada that Fraser was ill.

As Fraser tells in his narrative, he came home from Canada in February 1967. He had to be based near a major medical centre, first in Aberdeen and then in Edinburgh. The following section, from around that time, is told in Mother's own words.

Can a Mother Forget?

During the early stages of his illness, I looked after the shop in Dingwall during the week, but on Fridays I went down to be with Fraser for the weekend in Edinburgh. However, one night in the middle of the week in Dingwall, I woke up suddenly. I felt rigid, as if I was paralysed. I felt completely helpless, unable to move. I was gripped by a fear that I and my family were in danger and that there was nothing I could do about it. I tried to pray, I tried to go back to sleep, but I seemed unable to do anything. Then the words of Jeremiah 49:11 came to me: 'Leave your fatherless children, I will preserve them alive, and let your widows trust in me.' I relaxed completely, and went off to sleep after that.

At seven the next morning, I got a message from Edinburgh that Fraser had been taken into hospital. I said, 'I'll come down to Edinburgh right away.' But later that morning James phoned and advised me just to wait till Friday and come down then as I usually did. While I was speaking with him, the words which had meant so much to me during the night came back to me: 'I will preserve them alive.'

In September 1968 Fraser was in Raigmore Hospital in Inverness, after having suffered total renal failure. His blood urea was going up and up. He could not sleep. I stayed in the hospital with him one night, but it made no difference. He was desperately ill. One day Dr Knox took me away from the ward and we sat on a bench outside the hospital. He told me quite plainly that Fraser was not going to recover. When I went down to the town after that conversation, I felt completely stunned. I could not remember the way to the railway station, to catch a train to get back to Dingwall! I stood outside a shop window, pretending to be interested in what was on display, though not actually seeing anything. At last two ladies walked past, and I asked them if they knew the way to the station. They took me there. It was just round the corner from where I had been standing, in a daze.

After Fraser had been started on peritoneal dialysis, I was almost ill with worry about him. I would go along to the hospital, but sometimes I would be there for a whole visiting hour with him and he would not say one word. One time he said over and over again (you would hardly think it possible to get the words out so fast), 'Did I say to you that I did not know you? Did I say to you that I did not know you?'

I was coming back from the hospital one Sunday afternoon, walking across the Meadows towards Jean Nicolson's flat in Warrender Park Terrace, when I felt so tired I threw myself down on a park bench. I had been asking God that Fraser would either have a peaceful and joyful end, as his father had, or that he would get better. But at that point I felt depressed, unable to say a word to anyone. I asked the Lord what was the meaning of this – was he going to answer prayer?

That evening the Rev D. M. Macleod was preaching in Gilmore Place Church. (He was passing through Edinburgh at the time, on his way to New Zealand.) His text was Luke 24:50, about Jesus lifting up his hands and blessing his disciples as he was parted from them. I was in desperate need of help, and after the service the verse (especially the first line) from the Psalm came into my mind:

> *For yet I know I shall him praise,*
> *Who graciously to me*
> *The health is of my countenance,*
> *Yea, mine own God is he.*
>
> [Psalm 42:11]

After the service Mr Macleod asked if he could visit Fraser, and we arranged to go to the hospital the next day.

When we were climbing the stairs to the ward I said to Mr Macleod, 'Whatever is before us this verse is in my heart, "For yet I know I shall him praise".' He stopped on the stair beside me and said: 'These are the words of Scripture which came to me when I heard of Fraser's illness.'

We went on up the stairs and into the side room to put on sterile overclothes. Mr Robson, who was in charge of Fraser's treatment, happened to pass after visiting Fraser. I said to Mr Robson, 'This is a friend who is leaving for New Zealand and who would like to see Fraser.' He replied, 'You can go in for a minute, but he won't know you.'

Mr Macleod went in on his own and Fraser looked at him, held out his hand and asked, 'How are you, Mr Macleod?' When he came out after praying with Fraser he said, 'If I hadn't been told not to wait, I would happily have stayed in that room all day.'

There is a P. S. to the above. During that period, Fraser was not fit to read any of the letters which were arriving from different people, assuring him of their prayers on his behalf. But when he became stronger, he began to read them. One of the letters which he picked out was from Mr Macleod, who had by this time arrived in New Zealand. At the bottom of the letter Mr Macleod had written the words of that verse again, 'For yet I know I shall him praise.' It was like meeting an old friend. It reminded us that Fraser's survival was not just a natural thing. He was taken through that time because God took him through it, in fulfilment of the promise which he had given.

Three Memories

I was not so close to Fraser as Cameron was. But I remember standing beside his bed in the Edinburgh Royal Infirmary when he was at a very low point, and hearing him say, 'Take hold of my hand.' I felt it a privilege to be even of a little use, helping him through one of the many hours of pain which he was called to endure.

And I remember him preaching in Edinburgh, at some stage during his illness. Climbing the long stairs to the pulpit in Gilmore Place Church, he was the picture of weakness. The same man as I remembered flying round the sports track below Dingwall Academy in 1964 had to pause between each step going up to the pulpit in Edinburgh, just a few years later. His text was, 'Jesus wept.' Actually, I felt that his weakness enhanced the effectiveness of his presentation that day. He was physically incapable of racing on, packing in extra details, as he sometimes did. His delivery was like a film in slow motion. The impact, I thought, was quite remarkable.

And then I remember being in the study of the F. P. manse in Dingwall with the minister, the Rev. D. A. Macfarlane. (This is the minister to whom Mother referred, as being of help to her after he came to Dingwall in 1930.) It was now August, 1971. Fraser, like someone who had been raised from the dead, was about to be inducted to the Strath congregation in Skye.

'It's very remarkable,' Mr Macfarlane said, 'about Joseph.'

'What are you thinking of?' I asked. He looked at me as if I should have been able to read his thoughts without having them spelled out.

'Eh – in Genesis 39. I think it says three times there that "The Lord was with Joseph".' At this point Mr Macfarlane noticed that a large lump of coal was dangerously near the front of the grate, got up to tread on it firmly with his slipper, then went on: 'It tells about his brothers selling him down to Egypt, about poor Potiphar's wife and what she did, about Joseph being put in prison, and all that. But, in spite of everything, "The Lord was with Joseph". I think you'll find that it says that three times.'

As he said that last sentence, Mr Macfarlane turned away from the fire and looked over his glasses straight at me. The point came home to me that God had carried Joseph through various deep trials to serve him in happier circumstances, and

I thought also of the induction which was to take place in Skye later that week. I saw the connection, which had been so obvious to Mr Macfarlane, between the experience of Joseph and the fact that Fraser had been taken through years of severe illness and had been raised up again to begin a new ministry.

1971 *to* 1989

The fact that his health was not perfect did not keep Fraser from fulfilling every aspect of his subsequent ministry. He visited homes, and preached in different locations. Some-times he preached in Gaelic. Nor was he restrained from climbing on one occasion to the top of the Cuillins. Strictly speaking, he should have stayed down at sea level with most of the other inhabitants of Skye. One of the drugs he was taking to prevent rejection of his new kidney rendered his bones more liable to fracture. He did in fact break his ankle while he was up there, and had to be taken down by the Mountain Rescue services.

His ministry in Broadford lasted for eight years. Then, in 1979, he left to become minister of the F. P. congregation in Kinlochbervie and Scourie, Sutherland.

While he was in Kinlochbervie he began to suffer from heart trouble. He had to go to Edinburgh for a triple by-pass operation. For Mother, returning to Edinburgh to visit Fraser again in hospital was like a bad dream which had returned. Others who had had the same operation seemed to get better quickly, but Fraser was desperately ill. (He had actually caught 'flu while in hospital.) He felt sure that he was going to die. Mother, again staying with her life-long friend Jean Nicolson in her flat in Warrender Park Crescent, woke in the middle of one night and went through to the sitting room. Full of anxiety, she picked up a Bible and found that it opened for her at John chapter 11. She read the words, 'Did I not say to you that if you would believe you would see the glory of God?' She just accepted these words with the faith of a child, went back to bed and fell asleep at once.

While Fraser was in Kinlochbervie he astonished everyone in the community by covering the massive gable end of his manse with a painting of staggering size, colour and depth. Neighbouring children used to talk to him about it, and passing tourists would stop and ask him to explain its meaning. It included various symbols of spiritual significance, like the burning bush, threatened but never extinguished, and was featured on a television programme.

1989 to 1998

In 1989 a division occurred within the Free Presbyterian Church, mainly on matters relating to freedom of conscience. Fraser was among those who left the F. P. Church to form the Associated Presbyterian Churches. For the time being, he remained in Kinlochbervie and continued to minister to those in his congregation who shared his outlook. But in 1995 he moved to take up his final charge – the APC congregation of Wick, Thurso and Strathy in Caithness and Sutherland.

It was during these years that, despite failing health, he went off on a visit to Israel and Egypt in the heat of summer. He also travelled to visit APC congregations in New Zealand, though his health was so precarious that the travel company would not issue him with insurance cover. As 1998 progressed Fraser was troubled by a nagging cough and persistent exhaustion. The appearance was sinister but, while a diagnosis was not being offered, Fraser forced himself to carry on with his ministry. During this difficult period, Mother would at times resist the evidence of serious illness and at times accept it because of a verse which she felt was given to her, 'Father, I desire that they also whom you gave me may be with me where I am, that they may behold my glory which you have given me.'

Eventually, it was confirmed that Fraser was in fact suffering from cancer. Mother's response, still thinking of the verse from the seventeenth chapter of John, was, 'In many cases the will of God is unclear. But in this case it is made clear that Christ's will is for his people to be with him, and we have to yield to that. Of course it is sad, and of course we will miss him very much. Some people might think that we should be down about it and weeping. But we have to lean hard on God for all our strength.'

The fact that God did give Mother strength was very evident during these closing months of Fraser's life. For part of this time he was nursed in her home in Dingwall (although this would have been impossible without the support of her sister Helen, who lived nearby).

It was difficult to witness someone who was so committed to life and to freedom being dragged down. But Fraser did his utmost to make things easy for those who were suffering with him.

At one point Cameron, just before returning to Hong Kong, was visiting him in Mother's house. Fraser was about to be transferred to the hospice, but he did not focus on anything negative. 'I have been thinking of the words from the Epistle to the Philippians,' he said slowly, '*To me, to live is Christ and to die is gain.* The other day I saw that this points us away from the idea of death being an end which leads on to a new beginning. Life in Christ is a continuum, whether we live or whether we die.' It was with these uplifting thoughts that Fraser helped Cameron to face their final parting, and sent a brother to whom he owed so much away to catch a plane that would take him to the other side of the world.

From that same room in Mother's house in Blackwells Street, I remember another example of how Fraser helped us to view what was happening within a gospel framework. He was in the last stages of weakness. His face was like a mask, his eyelids heavy, his voice strained and without expression. Yet it regained a bit of bounce as he spoke of various verses of Scripture which had come into his mind earlier in the year. That was when he was sure that he was seriously ill, but over a long period it seemed that nothing was being done to establish the real nature of his illness. During this time he found that these Bible passages prepared him for what was to come. One was Psalm 121, on which Fraser commented, 'When you feel your feet sliding, it is good to know that "He will not allow your foot to be moved".'

Another verse was Psalm 73:26 (the text from which Fraser spoke at the last service which he took in Strathy): 'My flesh and my heart fail but God is the strength of my heart and my portion for ever'. He was sorry to be told of someone else who was distressed because of illness but he said that, for himself, 'It has been the opposite with me. I have been wonderfully upheld.'

One of the doctors attending him in Mother's house in Dingwall said, with a degree of bluntness which Fraser actually liked, 'Well, you are lying there and you know what is ahead of you, and yet you are remarkably calm about it all. How can you smile like that?' He told him. One of the nurses who cared for him there also expressed amazement at his peace of mind. Fraser spoke to her, too, about the strength and comfort which he was finding in the gospel at that time. Afterwards she said to us that she had never met anything like it in these circumstances.

At times, during that last difficult period of his life, he expressed the hope that he might yet be able to go home to finish some projects. But his basic desire was that God would be glorified, whether by his life or by his death.

When Fraser was eventually transferred to the Highland Hospice in Inverness, Mother still spent a lot of these final days and nights with him. She was with him throughout his last night, and when he passed away early on the morning of 3 November 1998.

The funeral was held in the Free Church, Dingwall, on 6 November, conducted by Fraser's co-presbyters of the Associated Presbyterian Churches. Fraser had ministered throughout his life in small congregations. Yet there, marking his passing, was a massive congregation made up of people from different churches and from none, all touched in different ways by his life and by his death. The singing of that congregation was unforgettable. The verse from Psalm 73, which had been a support to Fraser when he needed it, was more meaningful now than ever:

> *My flesh and heart doth faint and fail,*
> *But God doth fail me never:*
> *For of my heart God is the strength*
> *And portion for ever.*

20

In Loving Memory

(By Fraser's nephew, David Tallach)

In his book, Fraser speaks of mourning for his grandmother before she actually died. To some extent, I went through the same process in regard to him.

I heard that he was unlikely to get better in August 1998. I wrote the first of my poems, 'In Loving Memory', for him on that day, followed by several more in September. I have no doubt this preparation helped, even a little, to cushion the blow of his death in November. Although unable to attend his funeral, my empathy with him and others in the family was expressed through the poems. My work on this book, alongside the poems, is in tribute to Fraser and his remarkable life.

A Second Lease of Life

He could have died before I was born,
But his life was spared
By providence, and the donation
Of his brother Cameron's kidney.
Uncle Fraser's life was given back to him
In a very real way.

Had he not lived, he could not have
Taken me up behind the hill in Dingwall,
To climb trees and throw snowballs,
Or buy me ice creams on summer holidays,
Playing football in the park.
So we remember his extended life with gratitude.

The Sands of Time

The sands of time are sinking,
As Uncle Fraser himself once sang.
I remember the hourglass in the Kinlochbervie manse study,
Grainy moments pouring from one chamber to another.

Yellow sand like the beach at Oldshoremore,
Where this modest fisher of men lived.
He followed the man who walked on the water
To the harbour of his life's end.

Footprints left on a beach soon fade,
Filled by the next high tide,
Smoothed out like new linen,
Waiting for the mark of another generation.

He walked with me on the old Culloden Moor,
The bones of our ancestors lying in peace below,
Clashing swords and Gaelic war-cries laid to rest.
Soon now, he will join them.

Not for ever shall the grave have victory,
Nor his body always be interred in the cold ground.
On the Last Day, he shall arise and break the soil,
As his Lord broke death, arising perfect and new.

In Loving Memory

The taste of salt runs down my cheek,
Salt water like the slip-slapping tides
Rising and falling in the bay behind the manse
In Kinlochbervie, waves ebbing and leaving their mark.

His body went through rough and heavy seas
As he laboured for his life:
Pitching, tossing, but still living.
Even when he had the sign of a shipwreck.

He who bade the waves be still
Now calls his valiant sailor home.
The harbour lights for him are shining,
Guided by the hand of his life's pilot.

Even with conflict in our hearts
There is peace beyond our understanding.
Now we see but through a glass darkly,
Then we shall see face to face.

I still see him walking the hills,
Ageless and painless now,
Far beyond our shadowlands.

Amputation

Steady now, here comes the knife,
The agonizing chop of separation imminent.
So hard, the thought of that loss,
The gashed arteries weeping on the ground.
Still sometimes I can feel it there,
Beating and pulsing with a phantom life.

So painful at first,
To lose that precious unique part of me.
No doubt healing will come with time,
But for now it really hurts.

Grief

There is no doubting the sharp reality of grief.
It tears into you, eats inside you,
Until there is nothing but a shell.
We were not made to feel nothing
Like machines, devoid of soul.
It is right to grieve, fitting to remember with joy
The highlights of his life, restored 29 years ago.
Now he has crossed the river,
We who remain behind
Will always remember and love him.

Butterfly Country

Caterpillars munching on a green leaf
Ask what happened to their brother,
Why he left them in their little world,
Changed beyond their understanding.

He went far beyond the tree where they live,
Flying with great swoops of glorious wings,
Gathering with others like him
In a beautiful, unending field.

My Last Memory

I saw him sitting in a chair by his bed,
Almost as lively as he used to be,
Talking vigorously to a nurse.
Time pressing on me, to catch my train.
I knew for him, time would soon be no longer.

Presenting him with my latest poems,
Writing on people and places I knew and loved,
Only two minutes to say goodbye.
He gripped my hand firmly in appreciation.
I turned to go home to my parents,
Leaving him to await his Father's will.

Goodbye

No, no, it is not.
We are sure to see his face again
When we ourselves have crossed the river,
Emerging deathless on the other side.

Then we will not know sorrow,
Time a green leaf soon withered
In the gale of eternity.
There will be no night there.

21

Mother – The Last Lap

On the morning of Fraser's funeral Mother said, 'Lord, I am as weak as water, but help me to get through this day.' Afterwards she testified with gratitude that God had answered her prayer.

But there was an inevitable cost. It was natural that, at the age of 87, Mother should begin to show signs of wear and tear. Her memory began to go. She would become confused, and it was not safe for her to be on her own. Eventually she agreed to go, for a short time, to a home in Inverness. In fact, Ballifeary House was to become her home for the last two and a half years of her life. Here she received devoted, Christian care.

She would always give visitors the warmest of welcomes. But at times, especially in the evenings, she was not only confused but painfully aware of her own confusion.

Visiting a house in Cromarty at that time, I saw a photo of the senior pupils from Dingwall Academy, taken in 1927. To my utter amazement, hiding at the back (she was always self-conscious about being tall when she was young) was my mother at 16 years of age. I took this photo in to Inverness to show to her. She recognized many of the faces. When I expressed surprise she responded: 'Well, of course I remember her! She used to come to school with me on the train every morning from Strathpeffer to Dingwall.'

Some things did not change. She never lost her commitment to others. I was with her once when a lady approached who had recently been bereaved of her husband. Mother was able to relate to that situation immediately. Her warm smile was there, her identification with someone who needed encouragement. It was never difficult to have a conversation with her about the gospel, or to engage her interest in a situation which needed her prayers. She could phone in an evening when she was tired, confused and frustrated; but if there was some issue which needed prayer she would put aside her personal upset so as to focus on the needs of others. She could even mention it the following day as something whose importance she had grasped completely, and which she was committing to God in ongoing prayer.

In the summer of 2001, although her spirit remained strong, she seemed to be losing ground. Her appetite left her, and she became increasingly thin. Quite suddenly, or so it seemed, she was dying of cancer.

This Way to Glory

There was a lot of activity outside her bedroom window as builders worked to erect an extension to the Home. But, inside that room, the structure of her body was coming down. Helen, who had done so much for her during these last years, was constantly with her. James was often there. Cameron and his wife Ishbel, visiting Scotland that summer from Hong Kong, were able to spend time with her.

In some ways, she was the same as ever. She told me again, on 15 August, the story which she had told several times, about dusting the door of the Stornoway manse in 1959, feeling suddenly anxious about being left without Father, and being deeply comforted by the words from Psalm 23: 'Goodness and mercy shall follow me . . . '

> Think of the security in that. The goodness of God coming behind you and a provision before you that no one could take from you. Sometimes we do not lean on God's promises as we should, and we are the losers for that. But I was enabled just to take that promise and to lean on it.

By the beginning of the following week, her health had deteriorated dramatically. She could not take any food, and even a drink of water tended to make her sick.

Standing beside her bed, I could not but remember her standing beside Fraser's bed in the hospice the day before he died, almost three years before. She had been there in her weakness, in her old age, her frailty. But she was there in the totality of her commitment, saying what she could to encourage him on the very last lap of a long and painful race. Now, her own race was drawing to a close.

Early on Friday, 24 August, she became weaker. Helen read some Psalms to her, including Psalm 84. Mother repeated several times the words from verse 11: 'The Lord will give grace and glory.'

Earlier that week I had felt a kind of resentment rising against the forces which were taking her from us. Why should we be robbed of this person who had come through so much, in whom the grace of God had been so evident, who had spent a lifetime committing every member of the family to God in prayer? Then I realized that something was going on here which no one could stop. Not that this was a mere blind force of nature. This tide of death which was pulling her away was included in forces listed by Paul as being under the control of Christ, working for the benefit of believers (*1 Cor.* 3: 21–23).

So, that Friday morning, I reminded her of something which Dr Hugh Gillies, an intimate friend from Stornoway, once said: 'Christ has changed the character of death for the believer. Death is his friend now. Death says to the believer, *Come this way to glory.*'

Around lunch time, Mother was delighted to welcome our oldest brother Andrew and his wife Beth. That evening, though for long periods apparently withdrawn from her surroundings, her face repeatedly relaxed into smiles which were natural and sweet.

She died the next morning at 7.15 a.m.

The funeral service was held in Inverness on 28 August, in the Associated Presbyterian Church of which she had become a member in 1989. The following day her body was taken to Stornoway. Friends were there who warmly remembered both our parents, though Father's ministry in the town had ended over forty years before. So we laid them to rest together, who had lived in the love of many, and in whose love they had died.

Coming away from that spot I remembered the words, given to us by our mother for that difficult day of our father's funeral in January 1960: 'Arise and depart, for this is not your rest.' And I thought of the words from Augustine, 'There, we shall rest and we shall see. We shall see and we shall love. We shall love and we shall praise. Behold, what shall be in the end, and shall not end.'

We Praise God for His Grace

To return to something mentioned in 'A Word of Explanation', at the beginning of this book: Looking back over this material it struck me that, although the grace of God comes to us personally, it is not a private thing. It is a public statement which God makes, revealing the kind of God he is. He repeats this statement in different ways, speaking to each succeeding generation through what he does in the hearts and lives of those who believe in him.

So he put his grace into the heart of Dr Macdonald of Ferintosh, and as a result his preaching was blessed to Donald Duff. Then, in 1870, Donald Duff was enriched by Spurgeon's gracious company and by his powerful preaching. The point applies to Donald Duff himself, to his daughter Elizabeth, to his grandson Samuel, to his great-granddaughter (Mother) and to his great-great-grandson (Fraser). The grace of God, given to us, is not for us only. Others benefit too, and God is glorified in it all.

This thought is echoed by Don Robertson, originally from Tain in Ross-shire but now living in Vancouver, Canada. After Mother's death he got in touch to say:

> Thank you for letting us know of the departure of your loving Mother who is now with her Saviour and loved ones gone ahead. Your dear Mother was not just 'your' Mother, but 'a Mother in Israel'. She showed deep affection and spiritual concern for so many, including ourselves. We have been so very grateful for her ministry to us. We praise God for his goodness and grace.